Selected Poems
of
Luigi Pirandello

Poetry, perhaps more than any other art, evinces the power of language, of esthetic expression. Poetry, in fact, is the most intellectual art, the most precise, the closest to thought.

Luigi Pirandello
Fogletti

Selected Poems of Luigi Pirandello

☉ ☉ ☉

Translated by
George Hochfield

Italica Press
New York
2016

Copyright © 2016 by George Hochfield

ITALICA PRESS, INC.
595 Main Street, Suite 605
New York, New York 10044

Italica Press Poetry in Translation Series

All rights reserved. No part of this publication may be reproduced, stored in a retrieval system, or transmitted, in any form or by any means, electronic, mechanical, photocopying, recording, or otherwise, without prior permission of Italica Press. For permission to reproduce selected portions for courses, please contact the Press at inquiries@italicapress.com.

Library of Congress Cataloging-in-Publication Data
Names: Pirandello, Luigi, 1867-1936, author. | Hochfield, George, translator.
 | Pirandello, Luigi, 1867-1936. Poems. Selections. | Pirandello, Luigi, 1867-1936. Poems. Selections. English.
Title: Selected poems of Luigi Pirandello / Translated by George Hochfield.
Description: New York : Italica Press, 2016. | Includes bibliographical references and index.
Identifiers: LCCN 2016021022 (print) | LCCN 2016036474 (ebook) | ISBN 9781599103204 (hardcover : alk. paper) | ISBN 9781599103211 (pbk. : alk. paper) | ISBN 9781599103228 (E-Book)
Subjects: LCSH: Pirandello, Luigi, 1867-1936--Translations into English.
Classification: LCC PQ4835.I7 A2 2016 (print) | LCC PQ4835.I7 (ebook)
 | DDC
 851/.912--dc23
LC record available at https://lccn.loc.gov/2016021022

Cover Image: Olive Tree, © Italica Press Archives, 2016.

For a Complete List of
Italica Poetry in Translation
Visit our Web Site at
http://www.italicapress.com/index013.html

About the Translator

George Hochfield earned his doctorate in English at the University of California, Berkeley. His specialty was American literature, and he has published important works on Henry Adams and on New England Transcendentalism. As a translator from Italian he has published a memoir, *The Officers Camp* by Giampiero Carocci, and a novel, *Luisa and the Silence* by Claudio Piersanti. He was also the principal translator, in collaboration with Leonard Nathan, of the *Selected Poems of Umberto Saba* (Yale University Press, 2008). This work was a finalist for the 2010 Lewis Galantière award of the American Translators Association.

◉ ◉ ◉

To the memory of Mayflower
and of Benjamin Hochfield.

Contents

About the Translator	V
Introduction	XI
Acknowledgments	XIV
Select Bibliography	XV
from Mal giocondo / Troubled Joy	1
Romanzi V / Romanzi 5	2
Allegre I / Allegre 1	4
Intermezzo lieto I / Intermezzo Lieto 1	6
Momentanee / Momentanee	8
Triste / Triste	12
Solitaria / Solitaria	18
from Pasqua in Gea / Easter in Gea	21
Appendice a «Pasqua in Gea» / Appendix to "Easter in Gea"	22
from Elegie Renane / Rhenish Elegies	27
from Elegie Renane / from Rhenish Elegies	28
from Zampogna / Bagpipes	33
Come muore / How It Dies	34
Panico / Panic	36
Alberi soli / Solitary Trees	38
Gara / The Contest	40
Rondine / Swallow	42
Temporale estivo / Summer Storm	46
Vigilia / On the Eve	48
A gloria / To Glory	50
Dondolio / Swinging	52
Compenso / Recompense	54
Chi resta / Who Remains	56
Ritorno / The Return	58
Attesa / Waiting	62

from FUORI DI CHIAVE / OFFKEY   65
   Preludio / Prelude   66
   Ingresso / Entrance   70
   La mèta / The Goal   74
   Il pianeta / The Planet   76
   Credo / Creed   82
   Il tesoro / Wealth   86
   Vecchio avviso / An Old Notice   88
   Melbthal / Melbthal   90
   Primavera dei terrazzi / Springtime on the Terraces   96
   L'occhio per la morte / An Eye for Death   100
   Onorio / Onorio   102
   Stormo / Flight of Birds   104
   Sempre bestia / Always an Animal   106
   Chiú / To-whoo   106
   Meriggio / High Noon   108
   Guardando il mare / Looking at the Sea   108
   Convegno / A Meeting   110
   Leggendo la storia / Reading History   116
   Tormenti / Punishments   118
   Comiato / Envoi   120

POESIE VARIE/ VARIOUS POEMS (UNCOLLECTED)   123
   Il globo / The Globe   124
   Lieta / Feeling Good   126
   Amor sincero / Sincere Love   130
   Notte insonne / Sleepless Nights   132
   La via / The Way   138
   Alba / Dawn   142
   Esame (1895) / Examination (1895)   146
   Approdo / Landing   148
   Torna, Gesu! / Jesus, Come Back!   150
   Esame (1896) / Examination (1896)   154
   L'abbandono / An Ending   156
   Primo rintocco / First Chime   164
   Esame (1906) / Examination (1906)   168
   Tenui luci improvvise / Glimmerings   174
   Esame (1910) / Examination (1910)   182
   Il compito / My Duty   194
   Conversando (1) / Conversation (1)   196
   Conversando (2) / Conversation (2)   198
   Sveglia / Wakeup Call   198
   L'ultimo caffè / The Last Coffee   200

[Senza titolo] / [Untitled]	204
Improvvisi / Impromptus	206
NOTES	211
APPENDIX 1: From *Arte e coscienza d'oggi* / Art and Consciousness in Our Time	217
APPENDIX 2: An Autobiographical Letter (1914)	227
CHRONOLOGY	231
INDEX OF FIRST LINES — ITALIAN	233
INDEX OF FIRST LINES — ENGLISH	237

◉ ◉ ◉

Introduction

1

This is the first English translation of poems by Luigi Pirandello. Most of the poems have waited more than a century for such an undertaking, an especially curious fate in light of Pirandello's immense fame during his later years. But he was chiefly famous for his plays, not his poetry. References to him in the press, or in critical writings, almost always referred to him as "the dramatist." And he was not merely a dramatist of normal proportions; he was incredibly prolific, the author of more than forty plays, as well as seven novels, and hundreds of short stories. The poems seem to have been drowned in this great outpouring.

At the same time it's also true that Pirandello became a poet at an important moment in the history of European poetry. During the last years of the nineteenth century and the first of the twentieth a transition was taking place away from the traditional forms of poetry to what was called — and it still is — modernism. The phenomenon is so familiar, and has been so successful, that it hardly needs explanation. Its chief characteristics were a loosening of the old constraints resulting in varied rhythms and stanzaic patterns, banishment of rhyme, and diction tending toward the conversational and away from the pompous and abstract. All this left Pirandello behind. Born in 1867, he belonged to the nineteenth century in matters of poetic style. Sonnets are rife in his early books, and their rhymes are unfailing. It seems probable that these characteristics have played a part in persuading translators as well as critics and ordinary readers that the poems are not worth bothering about.

But if it is true that Pirandello persisted for some time in making use of the traditional forms of poetry, it's also true that his mind was alive to the currents of his age. And after all, he was a radical innovator on the stage. Even in his early work there are elements of differentiation: a personal voice, for example, even if somewhat flamboyant, as if delivered by an actor: "I ask for lies, deceive me if you can!" And a certain degree of experimentation is quite evident in the later poems, especially the uncollected.

2

In the autobiographical letter (see Appendix 2) written in 1914 but first published in a periodical in 1924, Luigi Pirandello gave a thumbnail definition of his outlook on life. It is a "very sad farce," he wrote, "because we have in ourselves, despite being unable to know how or why, or from whom, a necessity to deceive ourselves continuously with the spontaneous creation of a reality (one for each and never the same for all), which little by little we discover to be vain and illusory."

It would seem very likely that this pithy and suggestive statement must tell us a good deal about Pirandello's literary production. If life is a sad farce always subject to the necessity of self-deception, this must have an effect on the writer's art. What sort of effect? What are its implications or underlying assumptions so far as literature is concerned? Pirandello, it must be said, was essentially a cerebral artist. His writing was stimulated by his ideas. He was not much interested in the rough surfaces of life for themselves. He was interested, rather, in the conundrums of life. For example, what would happen to a man who, believed to be dead, tried to assume a new identity? What if a man discovered that his appearance to others was different from what he had supposed it to be?

Questions like these take for granted what is fundamental to Pirandello's outlook: reality is not a fixed and permanent structure embracing the individual life, but a projection outward by the individual toward an external world that exists but can be known only partially by the limited means available to the human powers of knowledge and imagination. Furthermore, the absence of an external structure means that all knowledge is relative. Individuals are free to elaborate their personal visions of reality, especially since there are no universal laws of reason by which to judge them.

Pirandello, in other words, is one of those nineteenth-century intellectuals for whom religion has faded before the advance of science, and this circumstance has not yet become a matter of casual acceptance. On the contrary, the relativism that replaced the certainty of religious faith was an event of the utmost significance for him. (Not, it should be said, because he had ever been a believer.) It meant the loss of social coherence and of humanity's central place in the universe, and above all the loss of all sense of purpose in life. Over and over Pirandello returns to this theme of purposelessness in the poems, which became the vehicle of his most personal expression. The absence of purpose leading to relativism is the reason for life's farcical quality. It is in those recurring images of coaches rushing to nowhere, of that darkness, and "void" from which humanity awaits the answer to its prayers. It is also in those increasingly frequent images of Nature, especially the trees — silent, indifferent, unconscious, enduring — the very antithesis of chaotic human activity. These poems reveal a somber and sensitive man, the dramatist, who, when the play is over and the curtain is drawn, comes to the front of the stage and addresses the audience directly.

George Hochfield

Acknowledgments

These translations go back to the turn of this century, when Leonard Nathan and I were working on the translation of Umberto Saba's poetry.

In intervals related to the uncertainty of publication, we discovered and experimented with the almost forgotten poetry of Luigi Pirandello. The differences between the two bodies of work were striking and intriguing to us, especially since the poets were almost exact contemporaries. So far as we could tell, neither ever mentioned the other, or perhaps even read the other. So the early pages of this book were a continuation of our interest in the beginnings of Italian modernism, and at the same time of an especially congenial collaboration. Also involved was Professor Nicolas Perella, who had helped us with Saba. But illness and death cut short their contributions, and the book had to be largely finished without them. Nevertheless, I owe them a special debt of gratitude.

Judith Slater made many useful suggestions chiefly related to diction. She also read and commented on the Introduction, as did my sister, Sylvia Hochfield. Anne Milano Appel helped solve a particularly knotty problem of interpretation. She also taught me how to make an electronic copy of the text.

SELECT BIBLIOGRAPHY

Bassanese, Fiora A. *Understanding Luigi Pirandello.* Columbia: University of South Carolina Press, 1997.

Bassnett-McGuire, Susan. *Luigi Pirandello.* New York: Grove Press, 1983.

Bentley, Eric. *The Pirandello Commentaries.* Evanston, IL: Northwestern University Press, 1986.

Biasin, Gian Paolo, and Manuela Gieri, eds. *Luigi Pirandello: Contemporary Perspectives.* Toronto: University of Toronto Press, 1999.

Bussino, Giovanni. "Pirandello's Personal Experience with Madness." *Canadian Journal of Italian Studies* 6.23 (1983): 21–38.

Campo, Michael R., Luigi Pirandello, and Alberto Moravia. *Pirandello, Moravia, and Italian Poetry. Intermediate Readings in Italian.* New York: Macmillan Co., 1968.

Caputi, Anthony Francis. *Pirandello and the Crisis of Modern Consciousness.* Urbana: University of Illinois Press, 1988.

DiGaetani, John Louis, ed. *A Companion to Pirandello Studies.* New York and Westport, CT: Greenwood Press, 1991.

Giudice, Gaspare. *Pirandello: A Biography.* Translated by A. Hamilton. London: Oxford University Press, 1975.

Pirandello, Luigi. *On Humor.* Translated by Antonio Illiano and Daniel P. Testa. Chapel Hill: University of North Carolina Press, 1974.

—. *Tutte le poesie.* Milan: Mondadori, 1982.

◉ ◉ ◉

FROM

Mal giocondo

Troubled Joy

Romanzi V

Il paese che un dí sognai, del mondo
inesperto e deì mali, su la terra
già lungo tempo lo cercai, fidente
nel vago imaginar che scorta m'era.
Molti paesi visitai deluso,
molti da lungi salutai fuggendo,
e su i lor tetti, declinante il giorno,
con la notte, la pace e il dolce inganno
sempre invocai dei sogni e il calmo oblio.
Ma per incerte vie, tra sassi e spine,
tacito andando nel desio pungente,
quanta parte di me viva lasciai!
Folle, e sperai; folle, ebbi fede. E solo
a i danni miei presiede ora crudele
la coscenza che mai, che mai dal suolo
in cui giaccio, menzogne pietose,
amor di donna o carità d'amico,
a rïalzarmi non varran — più mai.
Né a te, paese dei miei sogni novi,
ora piú credo; e tardi, ahimè, compresi
che vano era cercarti sotto il sole.
Se tristi grue pe 'l ciel fosco passare
vedea mesto, tra gli alberi battuti
da i primi venti d'autunno, in mente
io mi dicea: «Là giú, là giú, lontano,
nel bel paese dei miei sogni andranno,
ove eterna fiorisce primavera.»
E a lui credea n'andassero, portate
dal lungo vento, anche le foglie ai rami
strappate; a lui le nuvole e le vaghe
da i petti umani illusion fuggite...

Era follia, follia certo; ma dolce.

Romanzi 5

The land I once dreamed of, ignorant
of the world and its ills, I long searched
the earth for, trusting to the vague image,
that possessed me. I visited many lands
disappointed, bade many long farewells
as I fled. And when daylight faded into
night above their roofs, I always recalled
the sweet fantasy of peace and calm forgetfulness
of my dreams. But by uncertain paths, among
rocks and thorns, pressed on in silence
by irresistible desire, how much of my life
have I left behind! Folly, and I still hoped.
Folly, I had faith. And for all my losses
the cruel knowledge I now have won
is that never, never, from the earth on which
I lie will the comforting illusions of a woman's
love or a friend's generosity come to raise
me up — never. Nor in you, land of my dreams,
do I now believe, and late, alas, have I
understood that it is vain to look for you
under the sun. When I saw the melancholy
cranes fly past in the threatening sky,
among the trees whipped by the first
winds of autumn, I said to myself, "Out there,
out there, far away, they will go to the beautiful
land of my dreams where spring eternally
blooms." And carried away by the strong wind,
the leaves stripped from the trees went there too,
and the clouds, and the vague illusions
in flight from the human breast....

It was folly, folly to be sure, but sweet.

Allegre *I*

Chi mai vorrà comprare le mie nuvole?
Da l'Atlantiade nembi-adunatore,
m'ebbi in retaggio quante van pe 'l cielo
nuvole in giro.

Sappi, mi disse il dio, ch'esse son vacche
sparse pe i campi liberi de l'aria;
n'abbi custodia e cura: io te ne cedo
l'alto dominio.

Gran mercé, rispos'io, liberal nume:
ben largo io vedo è il dono. Ma le poppe
di quelle vacche non dàn latte, e vano
or premo e spremo.

Ereditato in vece avrei piú tosto
la tua sagacità fine in rubare
bovi ai pastori, e la facondia e il ratto
alato piede.

Che non mi starei ora, resupino
da mane a sera, afflitto aerimante,
il viaggio a seguir di tante vane
nuvole, vano.

Or sú, chi vuol comprare le mie nuvole?
Io de i doni del dio non fo mercato,
ma a gran derrata vendo e senza usura
l'aerea merce.

Ne consiglio ai filosofi l'acquisto,
al papa, ai re regnanti e decaduti,
agli amanti fedeli, ai sognatori,
ai mille illusi;

ed agli uomini onesti ed ai poeti,
specialmente: Potranno su le nuvole
vivere gli uni onestamente, e gli altri
di poesia.

ALLEGRE 1

Who'd like to buy my clouds?
From the Atlantean cloud-gatherer
I inherited as many of them
as roam the sky.

Look, the god said to me, they are cows
at loose in the open fields of air.
Protect and care for them. Over them
I grant you supreme dominion.

How great a favor, I answered, liberal lord.
The gift is generous indeed. But the udders
of those cows give no milk, and I grasp
and squeeze in vain.

I would have rather fallen heir
to your cleverness in robbing herdsmen
of their oxen, and your eloquence, your swift,
winged feet.

Then I wouldn't be lying flat on my back
from dawn to dusk, a worn-out aeromancer,
vainly trying to follow the flights of all
these aimless clouds.

Come now, who wants to buy my clouds?
I'm making no profit from the god's gift,
but sell at cost and interest free
the airy merchandise.

I commend them to philosophers,
to the pope, to monarchs reigning or dethroned,
to faithful lovers and to those who dream,
to all the hopeful fools

and to honest men, and to the poets
especially: they can live on clouds,
the first honestly, the others
by their poems.

Intermezzo lieto I

Naviga lenta pe i silenzi arcani
de la tranquilla notte, e l'ampio ascende
arco sidereo la crescente Luna.

Ne la piena letizia del suo lume
beate il corso per l'immenso cielo
seguono ondate nuvolette lievi.

Ma a tanta de le sfere alta quiete
l'infinita de l'acque sottoposta
distesa con fragor vasto risponde;

come al sognato de le genti umane
divino Eliso, ove ogni affetto è muto,
il perpetuo tumulto de la vita.

In vano il ciel su l'Inquieto eterno
il suo velo purissimo distende,
e tutto, in largo cerchio, lo ricinge;

Non ei s'acqueta; ma la terra muta,
indocil mostro, senza posa batte
e con perenne lamentanza afflige.

Anima umana, e tal sei tu. Perduta
ne l'infinita immensità dei cieli,
su breve terra, inestimabil parte,

t'agiti e fremi, e dei tuoi vani amori
pieno e degli odi tuoi vorresti il mondo,
né mai, che in tanto ciel, pensi, vanisce

del globo, ove ti stai, l'essere inane,
quasi profumi di maligno fiore
che dolorose al cielo apra le foglie.

Intermezzo Lieto 1

The crescent moon sails slowly in the arcane
silences of the peaceful night, as it ascends
the wide sidereal arc.

In the full beauty of its light
blessed waves of wispy cloudlets follow
its path across the boundless sky.

But to the profound quiet of the distant spheres,
the infinite expanse of waters below
responds with a thunderous crash,

just as in mankind's dream of divine
Elysium, where every affection is muted,
the perpetual tumult of life.

In vain the sky extends its pure
veil over the eternal restlessness
and draws all things together in a great circle.

But the sea is not calmed, a rebellious monster
it ceaselessly pounds the mute earth
and afflicts it with endless suffering.

And such are you, human soul. Lost
in the infinite immensity of the heavens,
on little earth, your precious part,

you bustle and fret and want to fill
the world with your vain loves and hates,
nor do you ever think that under the great sky

you will disappear from the globe, a futile
being, like the scent of an evil flower
that opens its woeful petals to the heavens.

Momentanee

IV

Ogni attimo che fugge m'ammaestra:
Assiduo indagator d'ignoti beni
sia tu. Ratto che il tempo mi balestra,
uomo o forza non è che piú m'affreni.
Or godi in fin che la tua vita è destra,
e ti pajano miel tutti i veleni
che suggerai, come ape industriosa,
nel giardin de la vita dolorosa.

Ogni ideale è in van s'egli t'impaccia,
e stolto sei se mai d'un ben ti privi
per un rispetto sociale. Straccia
le leggi; tu l'hai scritto, e tu mentivi.

X

Fuggono i giorni miei sí come accolti
in un momento, e un'acerbezza dura
solo nel cuor mi lasciano, ché molti
quasi fuor d'ogni vita, in vana cura,
ne ho di già spesi inutilmente, e corto
cammin prescrisse ai giorni miei natura.
Dàmmi tu pace, amor, dàmmi conforto:
menzogne io chiedo, e ingannami se puoi!
Entro il cervello un mondo vano porto...
A te mi lega innanzi che m'ingoj
il vortice fatale, o pia fanciulla:
Un sogno ancora, una menzogna, e poi
la nera e fredda eternità del nulla.

Momentanee

4

Each fleeting moment teaches me:
be thou a tireless quester after unknown
pleasures. Time speeds me with its crossbow,
no man or force can longer hold me back.
Enjoy at last that your life is active
and may all the poisons you suck in,
like an industrious bee in the doleful
garden of life, seem to you like honey.

Every ideal is vain if it confines you,
and you're a fool if ever you deny yourself
a pleasure out of conformity. Tear up
the laws: you wrote them and you lied.

10

My days slip by as if gathered
into one moment, and they leave only
a grim bitterness in my heart,
for I have already squandered so many
of them uselessly, and nature
has ordained that my days will be few.
Tell me, thou, of peace, my love. Comfort me.
I ask for lies, deceive me if you can!
In my brain I carry an empty world....
Bind me to you before the fatal
vortex swallows me, O faithful girl.
Still one more dream, a lie, and then
the cold, black eternity of nothingness.

XV

Sono, io dico, come un uomo che si sia
lentamente rinvenuto,
dopo un lungo tra memorie dolorose
angosciare, e al fin respira.

Sono come senza meta un viandante
che, da fiero turbin colto,
scampa al vento, che ruggendo l'ha stordito,
sotto un tetto abbandonato.

Non memorie, non dolori. Sono in preda
a un confuso stupor vago,
levemente di lontani dolor conscio,
di lontani desiderî.

E un fantastico stupor di sogni strani
ho negli occhi, e parmi al guardo
una luce fresca e mite allerghi il cielo
oltre i limiti visivi.

15

I say that I am like a man who has
slowly revived
from a long agony among painful
memories, and at last can breathe.

I'm like an aimless wayfarer
who, caught in a fierce squall,
takes refuge from the howling wind that has
bewildered him under an abandoned roof.

Not memories. Not sorrows. I am prey
to a vague, confused stupor,
faintly conscious of a distant pain,
of distant desires.

And in my eyes there is an awestruck
vision of strange dreams, and beyond
my sight a pure light and peaceful shelters
unseen in the heavens.

TRISTE

II

Ecco la folla. — Chierici e beoni,
giovani e vecchi, femine ed ostieri,
soldati, rivenduglioli, accattoni,
voi nati d'ozio e di lascivia, serî
uomini no, ma pance, lieti amanti,
bottegaj, vetturini, gazzettieri,
voi vagheggini, anzi stoffe ambulanti,
donne vendute da l'inceder franco,
goffe nutrici, e voi dame eleganti,
quale strano spettacolo a lo stanco
di rimirar, non sazio, occhio offerite
così male accozzate in largo branco.
Oh viaggio curioso de le vite
sciocche d'innumerabili mortali!
Oh per le vie de le città spedite,

che retata di drammi originali!...

III

Godi, o mia carne, fino a che perdura
de gli anni il giovanil baldo vigore;
vivi senza legami, e sol procura
che il rider troppo non ci spezzi il cuore.
Viltà, la passione. Età matura
non a lento ne strugga, in reo torpore;
dieci anni ancora, e ci trarrem la cura
di vivere senz'odio e senza amore.

Oltraggia il tempo; e i vecchi odio, che senza
una speranza, in tedio, egri, per via
trascinano la propria decadenza;
noi, morti ai godimenti, avrem riposo,
e ti darò a la terra, o carne mia,
perché rinasca in fungo velenoso.

TRISTE

2

Look at this crowd: priests and drunks,
young and old, women and publicans,
soldiers, hawkers, beggars;
you who were born of idleness and lust, not
real men, no, bellies; complacent lovers,
shopkeepers, cabmen, hack reporters,
and you gigolos, or rather walking suits,
women for sale with their brazen strut,
clumsy wet-nurses, and elegant ladies —
what a fantastic spectacle you offer the weary
but unsated eye to gaze upon, rudely
thrown together in a great crowd.
Oh strange caravan of the absurd
lives of innumerable mortals!
Oh, you surge through the cities' streets,

what a bounty of original dramas!…

3

Take pleasure, oh my flesh, as long as the years
of vigorous youth may last.
Live without chains, and only make sure
too much laughter doesn't break your heart.
Passion is cowardly. Mature age
quickly consumes it in guilty torpor.
After ten years it will take from us the fear
of living without hate and without love.

Time degrades, and I hate the old who
hopeless, in boredom and infirmity, drag
their decay through the street.
We, dead to pleasure, will have rest,
and I will give you to the earth, oh my flesh,
to be reborn as a poisonous mushroom.

VIII

Sono a la mia finestra, al quinto piano,
e guardo giú per via: — C'è molto fango;
oggi non scenderò. — Nubi vaganti,
nubi ideal d'ogni ideale vano,
nubi amor dei poeti e degli amanti,
egli è dunque cosí che va a finire
l'alta idealità che vì sublima?
Ahimè tutto quel fango, altere nubi,
(colla che i piedi attacca dei mortali
a questa enorme trottola sciocchissima
per gli spazî lanciata a raggirarsi
in eterno) da voi, da voi diviene.
Oggi non scenderò: Socchiudo gli occhi,
e mi pare d'assistere da l'alto
ad un sedizioso di formiche
commovimento. Oh via! Formiche.... È troppo:
Chi mi dice che giú, tra tanta gente
non possa a un tratto capitare un qualche
grand'uomo? È ben probabile: in Italia,
al dì d'oggi i grand'uomini si contano
a centinaja di migliaja, e ovunque
se ne incontrano, e sempre. Quando meno
te l'aspetti, t'imbatti, a mo' d'esempio,
in un che a prima vista un onest'uomo
diresti — e bene — trema — egli è quel tale
poeta, o mettiamo, quel pittore,
quello scultor di cui parlò pur jeri
tutto il mondo — e l'han fatto senatore.
Ma un cane oggi non v'è che lo rammenti.
— Buona gente, fermatevi un istante
sotto la mia finestra, e udite, udite:
Ho perduto tra voi, come si perde
una berretta o una parrucca, il mio
cervello e de la vita il vero scopo.
Ora, a voi: Getto quanto mi rimane

8

I'm at my window on the fifth floor,
and I look down at the street: there's lots of mud.
Today I won't go out. Drifting clouds,
the images of every vain ideal,
clouds, beloved of poets and of lovers,
is this, then, what it comes to,
the lofty idealism that exalts you?
Alas, all that mud, noble clouds,
(which glues the feet of mortals
to this huge ridiculous top
hurled into space to spin
eternally) comes from you, from you.
Today I won't go out. I narrow my eyes
and seem to witness from above
a riotous commotion of ants.
Oh come now! Ants.... That's too much.
Who says that down below, among so many people,
some great man cannot turn up
at any time? It's very likely: in Italy
nowadays great men are counted
in the hundreds of thousands and can
be met with everywhere and all the time. When you
least expect it, you'll meet, for instance,
one who at first sight you'd think an honest man,
and, by God — you may well tremble — he is
that poet, or let us say, that painter,
that sculptor, of whom just yesterday
all the world was talking, and they've made him senator.
But not even a dog remembers him today.
— Good people, stop a moment
under my window and listen, listen:
I have lost among you, as one might lose
a cap or wig, my mind, and the true end of life.
Now, I fling to you all that's left to me

in sen d'affetti: amore, odî, speranze,
desiderî, virtù, vizî, ogni cosa,
e il vile ossequio che prestai per tanto
tempo a le vostre leggi! A voi: Dal viso
la maschera, or compunta or gioviale,
mi strappo — e ve l'avvento: La portai
già troppo; e sol con essa vi baciai...
Raccattatela or voi — vi farà ancora
un benevolo ed ultimo sorriso,
e vi dirà: «Buon dí, cari fratelli;
Dio vi conservi lungamente sani».
Tutto, tutto vi getto, onesta gente;
ma i miei pensieri no — sarebber pioggia
di ciottoli roventi su di voi.
Fango e menzogna costà giú s'impasta,
e novi figli crescono a la patria.
Io sto, qui, in alto. — O centenarî corvi,
che raccogliete il vol su i campanili
de le romane chiese, e accoccolati
su le croci di ferro o su le teste
de le marmoree sante, ruminate
di tanti anni gli eventi e i fasti novi
di questa eterna Roma; a voi do in pasto,
neri corvi, il cuor mio. Sú, sú, volate
e gracchiate, e gracchiate a piena gola,
da un capo a l'altro la città correndo,
ciò che del mondo e ciò che de la vita

un illuso pensò. — Chiudo le imposte.

of feelings in my breast: love, hate, hope,
desire, virtue, vice, everything,
and the base respect I gave your laws
for so long! For you: I tear the mask
from my face, now rueful, now good humored,
and hurl it at you. I've worn it
too long, and only with it on I kissed you...
Now gather up its shreds — it will yet give
a last and kindly smile,
and say to you, "Good day, dear brothers.
God keep you well for a long, long time."
Everything I have I throw to you, good people,
but my thoughts, no: they would rain down
like burning cobblestones.
Mud and lies are mingled there below,
and new sons grow up for the fatherland.
I stay here, above it all. — O ancient crows
that gather in flight on the bell towers
of the Roman churches and, squatting
on the iron crosses or the marble
heads of saints, ponder the events of so
many years and the new pomps
of this eternal Rome: to you, black crows, I give
my heart as food. Up, up, fly
and croak, croak as loudly as you can,
racing from one end of the city to the other,
what a dreamer thought of the world

and of life. I close the blinds.

SOLITARIA

   Eterno immenso e vario
comporre un canto solo, e tutta in quello
chiuder l'anima, come in uno snello
   bel vaso cinerario:
questo vorrei; ma de l'umane genti
raccoglier pria, perché il perenne canto
tragga voce da loro e vivi accenti,
i pensieri e gli affetti e gli odî e il pianto.
Questo. Ed a te, profonda notte, in vano
su noi pregata senza dipartita,
dire co 'l poderoso canto umano
la vanità de l'essere infinita.

Solitaria

   This I would do: compose a single ode,
vast, eternal, many-faceted,
and close in it the soul as in a perfect,
   slender cinerary urn,
but first I'd gather up from human beings,
their thoughts and feelings, hates and griefs,
so that the immortal song might draw
from them its voice and living accents.
And then to you, bottomless night, in vain
prayed to above us but never dispelled,
with the mighty human song I would tell
the infinite vanity of being.

FROM

Pasqua in Gea

Easter in Gea

Appendice a «Pasqua in Gea»

«*Eterno eterno eterno!*»
susurran l'aure in torno,
quasi oppressanti. «*Eterno!*»
ripete il vasto Reno
fluendo senza posa.
«*Eterno eterno eterno!*»
chiede ogni viva cosa.
Io vo, sconvolto il seno
da un rompere improvviso
d'affetti novi, pieno
d'accese idee la mente;
non lieto, e pur ridente
di strani sogni il viso.
Dove? io non so, ma avanti —
verso la morte, forse;
forse in braccio a l'amore;
saprò forse tra poco
il gran Secreto. Avanti!
Non mai sí ratto corse
su noi lo stuol de l'ore;
non mai sí viva apparve
ad occhio uman la terra;
né mai con tanto foco
vegliaronla le stelle.
Questa è magica sera;
questo, novel ritorno
di gaja primavera
sarà per me fatale.
In van le antiche larve
di nostra poesia,
e de le forme belle
l'armonïosa vita
chiama a compor la guerra
dei paventosi affetti
la vaga fantasia.

Appendix to "Easter in Gea"

"Eternal eternal eternal!"
the air whispers it everywhere
almost stiflingly: "Eternal!"
repeats the vast Rhine
flowing without pause.
"Eternal eternal eternal!"
cries every living thing.
I am, my breast shaken
by a sudden burst
of new feelings, my head
full of radiant thoughts,
not happy, and yet my face
laughing with strange dreams.
Where to? I don't know, but onward,
toward death, perhaps,
perhaps on the arm of love;
perhaps I will soon know
the great Secret. Forward!
Never again will the wealth of hours
be stolen from us by haste.
Never again will the earth
look so alive to human eyes,
or will the stars come out
with so much brilliance.
This is a magical evening,
this new return
of joyful Spring
will be my destiny.
In vain the ancient ghosts
of our poetry
and of the beautiful forms
of harmonious life
cry out to settle the war
of frightened feelings,
the vague imagination.

*Qui è 'l coro trïonfale,
il formidabil coro
de le reali forme,
possenti ne la loro
integrità vitale.
Qui l'anima è rapita
dal grande multiforme
trionfo degli aspetti;
e preso a forza io sono
e a tutto m'abbandono,
e del tutto divento:
Mortal cosa non scrivo,
che l'infinito io sento,
sento l'eterno — e vivo.*

Here is the triumphal chorus,
the formidable chorus
of the true forms,
powerful in their
vital integrity.
Here the soul is enthralled
by the great multiform
triumph of appearances,
and I am forcibly held
and abandon myself to all,
and I become part of all.
I do not write a time-bound thing
for I sense the infinite,
I feel the eternal — and I live.

FROM

Elegie Renane

Rhenish Elegies

from Elegie Renane

Del forestier che ancora il sol della patria ha negli occhi
e oppresso qui della natura ingrata

vive solingo al fuoco, udendo attraverso la gola
fumida del camino gemer continuo il vento,

tenera e premurosa, tu cura ti prendi fraterna:
l'ore con lui dividi, tacite sieno o gaje.

Cuci, mentr'egli scrive. Dai candidi lini e dal foglio
levansi e si sorridon gli occhi di tratto in tratto.

Giú per la scala di legno, furtiva a lui scendi la notte.
Tremi e nel pronto amplesso soffochi la paura.

Ei nell'attesa il bujo paventa, ché attorno, anelando,
ispido di rimorso, gelido e reo lo sente.

Teco la vita viene, a cui non sa chiuder le braccia,
egli, per quanto questo pungolo interno senta.

Come potrebbe dirti: «Ritorna al tuo gelido letto»,
se tu la gioja delle fiorenti membra

vieni a portargli e scendi a lui che t'aspetta, volente?
e quest'amor per te piú d'ogni cosa vale?

Non ei promessa alcuna t'ha fatta. E pur pensa: «Domani,
se quest'amore spezzo, che avverrà mai di lei?»

Già ti vede perduta, e interroga i cogniti luoghi,
quale, per te diserta, funebre aspetto avranno.

Mentre del sol le parlo d'Italia, i cari occhi socchiude
languida, e su le membra par che il ristor ne senta.

FROM RHENISH ELEGIES

Of the foreigner who still has the sun of his homeland
    in his eyes,
  and here is oppressed by hostile nature,

who lives alone by the fire, hearing from the smoky
  throat of the chimney the continual moan of the wind,

gentle and considerate, you care for him like a brother.
  You share the hours with him, quiet or joyous.

You sew while he writes. From white linens and from pages
  eyes are raised and smile from time to time.

You come down to him secretly by the wooden staircase
    at night.
  You shiver and in a quick embrace you stifle your fear.

As he waits, the surrounding darkness frightens
    him, breathless,
  irritable with remorse, he feels ice cold and guilty.

Life comes with you, he cannot close his arms
  however much he feels this inner pang.

How could he tell you, "Go back to your cold bed,"
  if you come to bring him the pleasure of healthy

limbs, and you come down willingly to him who awaits you?
  If this love is worth more to you than anything else?

He has made no promises to her. And he thinks: "Tomorrow,
  if this love is dashed, what will ever be true for her?"

Already he sees you lost and questioning the familiar places,
  which, deserted by you, will have a gloomy look.

While I talk to her of Italy and its sunshine, her
    dear eyes languidly
  half-close, and she seems to feel her body refreshed.

*Vede attraverso le mie colorite parole i tre mari,
vede città ridenti, vede campagne e piagge.*

*Godo cosí, sospesa, smarrita lontano, su l'ali
della mia visione l'anima sua guidare.*

*Poi d'un tratto (son io pure Italia per lei)
qua con un grido e un bacio, trepida la richiamo.*

She sees through my vivid words the three seas,
  she sees smiling cities, countryside, and beaches.

Thus I find pleasure, suspended, wandering far,
  leading her soul on the wings of my vision.

Then suddenly (it's I who am Italy for her)
  with a cry and a kiss, anxiously I call her back.

FROM

Zampogna

Bagpipes

Come muore

Ecco, a un mandorlo appende
il suo mantel di neve
l'inverno che già muore....
Il mantel bianco e lieve
su i rami si rapprende,
ed ogni grumo è un fiore.

Steso del tronco a piede
guarda l'inverno in sú
con occhi acquosi, intento.
Farfalle o fior? Non vede
il suo mantelo piú....
S'adira, soffia: il vento

è solo un debil fiato,
agita i fiori appena....
E un'altra, un'altra pena
la sorte gli riserba:
muor tutto fili d'erba!
il crin, la barba, un prato....

How It Dies

   Look, winter, already dying,
hangs on an almond tree
its coat of snow.
The coat, white and thin,
congeals on the branches,
and every clot is a flower.

   Stretched out from the trunk,
winter gazes up
with watery eyes, intent.
Butterfly or flower? He sees
his coat no more.…
This angers him, he huffs, the wind

   is only a feeble breath
that barely stirs the flowers.…
And another, a new blow
fate has in store for him:
he dies all blades of grass!
the mane, the beard, a pasture.…

Panico

Pe 'l remoto viale di campagna,
tra fitte macchie, in sul cader del giorno:
io solo. È tal silenzio tutto intorno
che a un ragno sentirei tesser la ragna.

Come si tien cosí sospesa tanta
vita di foglie? Il cuore anch'io mi sento
sospeso, oppresso da strano sgomento;
stupito or questa guato or quella pianta.

L'anima quasi al limitar dei sensi
scende ansiosa, ma alcun lieve moto
non coglie, alcun rumore, e come un vuoto
mi s'apre dentro. Penetra fra i densi

rami del sol l'ultimo raggio intanto
e accende in alto lumi d'oro strani
nella macchia dei bigi ippocastani
che un tempio sembra ed opera d'incanto.

Di questa intimità con la natura
solitaria, del tutto inconsueta,
l'anima mia divien tanto inquieta,
quanto sarebbe forse per paura.

De' suoi sacri silenzii ancor non degno
dunque son io. Ma di notturne brine
tanto mi bagnerò che, puro alfine,
ella accoglier mi possa in questo regno.

Panic

   On a remote country path,
among dense brush, at the close of day,
I am alone. There is such stillness all around
that I could hear a spider spin its web.

   How does the teeming life of leaves
suspend itself? I feel my heart
suspended too, oppressed by strange dread.
Dazed, I stare now at this, now at that shrub.

   Anxiously my soul descends almost to
the threshold of the senses, but not the slightest stir,
not a sound, does it take in, and something opens
in me like a void. Meanwhile, the sun's last ray

   penetrates the dense branches
igniting eerie golden lights
high in the foliage of the ashen chestnut trees
that seem a temple and a work of magic.

   By this solitary intimacy
with nature, wholly beyond the usual,
my soul is as shaken as it would
have been, perhaps, by fear.

   Then I am still unworthy of her sacred
silences. But I will bathe myself
in the dews of night until, finally pure,
she will receive me into this realm.

Alberi soli

    O castagni del bosco, un altro cielo
tutto di foglie tremule tessuto
voi, snelli e dritti sul cinereo stelo,
formate sul mio capo: ognun di voi
        presso l'altro cresciuto,
come sia triste ignora e quanto annoi
vedersi solo, sentirsi sperduto...
Fra voi ripenso a tre alberetti grami
che, traversando la maremma in treno,
vidi una notte. Bassa, dietro un velo
di nebbia, era la luna. I loro rami
congiunti avean quegli alberi e la trista
sorte d'essere nati in quel terreno:
si tenean compagnia fra loro stretti,
        lì, come tre vecchietti;
e parea che volessero la vista
sfuggir d'un altro alberetto lontano
un buon tratto da loro e solo solo.
    Tendeva questo invano
i rami verso i tre fra loro uniti;
e chi sa quanti uccelli aveano il volo
di questo a quelli spiccato a recare
        querelle amare e inviti...

Solitary Trees

    O chestnut trees in the woods, you make
another sky above my head, woven all
of trembling leaves. Slender and straight
on your ashen trunks, each of you
        has grown beside the others.
How sad to be neglected and how troubling
to know oneself alone, to feel cut off....
Here among you I recall three pitiful little trees
I saw one night when crossing the coastal
marsh by train. The moon was low
behind a veil of mist. The branches
of these trees were meshed, like their sad
fate of being born in that terrain.
They kept close company there among themselves,
        like three old men,
and it seemed they wished to flee
the sight of another tree some distance
from them and all alone.
        This one vainly stretched
its branches toward the close-knit three,
and who can tell how many birds had flown
from it to them, chosen to convey
        bitter grievances and invitations....

GARA

Gli alberetti di mandorlo, piccini,
studiano i grandi, come vengan sú,
e come questi atteggiano i lor fini
ramicelli e i polloni; ed or che giú
per il declivo de l'aperta valle,
con tanti fior che pajono farfalle
qualche grande han veduto, inuzzoliti,
per imitarlo, poveri alberetti,
tra lo scherno dei passeri folletti,
di bianche lumachelle son fioriti.

The Contest

The little almond trees, the saplings,
study the big ones, how they rise,
and how they display their slender
delicate limbs and shoots, and having seen,
on the slope of the open valley,
some of the big ones full of blossoms
that look like butterflies, they long
to emulate them, pathetic little trees.
Amid the mockery of impish sparrows
they have bloomed with small white snails.

Rondine

Volle pe 'l nido suo, pei nati suoi,
ghermir la piuma aerea che il fanciullo
con una canna le tendea. Fu poi,
legata per un piede, anche trastullo
d'ogni gente per casa. Al fin, sorpreso
il momento opportuno, un guizzo sbieco,
e via, per la finestra, a vol: ma un peso
l'ali le aggrava: il lungo laccio ha seco.

Un punto solitario alto lontano
cercò dal ciel l'acuta sua pupilla.
Le mancava la forza e già sul piano
ruinava... Sú, sú, nel sole brilla
in cima al monte prossimo e s'avventa
fremendo all'aure un albero: lassú! —

E qui sul nodo al piede a lungo intenta
col becco s'ostinò.

— Faggio, oh ma tu,
tu che, felice, a questo monte in vetta,
da un secolo coi venti ampii conversi
e, nell'altera libertà, vedetta
e prima meta a gli stanchi, ai dispersi
stormi di passo da tant'anni sei;
tu che i migranti all'ultimo convegno
raccogli; non dovevi a gli occhi miei
lo spettacolo offrir lugubre, indegno
di te: codesta rondine a un tuo ramo
appesa, spenzolante...
Ella, lo so,
malcauta prima, come boga all'amo,
si appese; qui da sé poi s'intricò:
ma si credea già libera saltando
pe' rami tuoi frondosi, fino a sera;

SWALLOW

   She wanted for her nest, for her newborns,
to snatch the airy feather that the boy
held out to her with a stick. Then, she was
tied by a foot, the sport
of all the household. At last, seizing
an opportune moment, a sidelong dart,
and out the window she flies; but a weight
bears down her wings, the long noose clings to her.

   From the sky her keen eye searched
for a solitary point, high and remote.
She was losing strength, already she fell
toward the plain.... Up, up, on the summit
of a nearby mountain, gleaming in the sun,
a tree, fluttering in the wind, and she hurls
herself toward it — up there!

And she works at the knot with her beak
intently and for a long time.

       Oh but you, beech tree,
who, happy on this mountain peak,
converse for a century with the wide winds
and, in proud liberty, are lookout
and first destination of the weary, the scattered,
passing flocks for so many years,
you where migrants gather for their last
meeting, you should not have made me
see a spectacle of grief unworthy
of you: that swallow hung from one
of your branches, dangling....
       She, I know,
heedless at first, like a fish with a hook,
caught herself, then became entangled,
but she believed herself already free, springing
among your leafy branches until dusk.

*forse ajuto pregò, misera; e quando
volaron gli altri uccelli, prigioniera
si vide in te di nuovo. E tu, tu solo
gridar la udisti, è ver? tutta la notte:
l'ali sforzava, rattenuta, al volo...
Finché non tacque, estenuata.
       Rotte
dal disperato sforzo e abbandonate
all'aria or l'ali pendono. Strisciando
piú rondini dall'alba son passate
a dimandare: "Com'è stato? Quando?"*

Perhaps she begged for help, poor thing, and when
the other birds flew by, she knew herself a prisoner
again in you. And you, you alone
heard her cry out, true? All night long
the wings held back, struggled to fly....
Until she lost her voice, exhausted.
                              Broken
by the desperate strain, the wings
now dangle loosely in the air. Skimming by
at dawn some swallows passed,
asking, "How did it happen? When?"

Temporale estivo

I. *(bróntola)*

Ride bagnato, addosso a la montagna,
il borgo al temporal che or or si muta
altrove, in giú, verso l'ampia campagna,
col suo tendon di pioggia fitta e acuta;

rapido gli altri borghi vi guadagna
e a suo modo col tuon pria li saluta.
Qui odor di terra e l'acqua che ristagna
per rispecchiare il ciel donde è caduta.

Burbero un nuvolon brontola ancora,
dal temporal quassú lasciato indietro:
patir non sa che scomodato il vento

l'abbia per cosí poco: al suo scontento
sol però si commove ad ora ad ora
tra le bacchette mal commesso un vetro.

II. *(gràcida)*

Ora gli alberi folti del viale
riversano, se l'aura un po' li mova,
a scosse, crepitanti, giú la piova
che hanno accolta testé dal temporale.

E il tufo arsiccio immollano, dal quale,
se è ver qual sembra, una famiglia nova
di girini qua e là saltanti scova
a cui fu l'acqua spirito vitale.

E saprà d'acqua il gracidío sonoro,
allor che divenuti raganelle,
nel silenzio, al pio lume de le stelle,

su questi rami canteranno a coro,
e le udrà grato nelle algenti sere,
tornando al borgo alpestre, il carrettiere.

SUMMER STORM

1. (it mutters)

   Drenched, the town perched on the mountain
   laughs at the storm below, now changing
   its course toward the sweeping countryside,
   with its canopy of dense and stinging rain.

   It quickly overtakes the other towns,
   greeting them in its way with thunder first.
   Here, the smell of earth, and pooled water
   that reflects the sky from where it fell.

   Gruffly a thundercloud, left behind
   by the storm, mutters again,
   impatient that the wind has disturbed him

   for such a little thing. At his annoyance,
   however, only a window rattles from time
   to time in its badly fitting frame.

2. (it croaks)

   Now the thick trees along the road,
   with the slightest movement of the air,
   pour down the rain, rattling and in spurts,
   that they have gathered from the storm.

   They make a sacrifice to the parched
   tufa, where if what seems to be is true, a new family
   of tadpoles, hopping here and there, is started,
   to whom the water was a vital spirit.

   And then, when they've become tree frogs,
   singing in chorus from the branches of trees,
   the carter, hearing their loud croaking

   in the silence, under the holy light
   of stars, will think with gratitude of water, coming
   home to the mountain town in the cold night.

VIGILIA

Appena qualche foglia, ad ora ad ora,
nei mandorli si muove sornuotanti
a un mar di messi che nel sol s'indora.

Nessun uccello in tanta pace vola;
sol laggiú le calandre saltellanti
trillano con la gioja nella gola.

E qui, tra il grano, par che un grillo metta
un frullo d'ali, a tratti. Oggi è per voi,
messi, l'ultimo dí: l'aja vi aspetta.

Sarà grano per noi, come ogni frutto
di quest'alberi qui sarà per noi
e quel degli orti e quel dei prati: tutto.

Chi maledir può qui la terra? Il canto
degli uccelli, — Ti siam grati, — le dice, —
Or sei stanca, riposa: hai fatto tanto.

E riposa la terra e par felice.

ON THE EVE

   Only a few leaves, from time to time,
floating down from the almond trees
to a sea of grain turning gold in the sun.

   No bird flies in all this peace,
only the larks hopping on the ground
and trilling with joy in their songs.

   And here, in the grain, a cricket begins,
now and then, a whir of wings. Today is your
last of harvest, grain: the threshing floor awaits you.

   There will be wheat for us, as for us
all the fruit of these trees
and of the gardens and the meadows: all.

   Who can speak ill of the earth? The birds'
song: "Our thanks to you," they tell her,
"now you're tired, rest. You've done so much."

   And the earth rests and looks happy.

A GLORIA

Un morto, e la campana non si lagna:
squilla, argentina, a gloria. Un bimbo, è vero?
entra in quest'alto e bianco cimitero
che ha, sotto, il mare e, dietro, la campagna.

Non ha mangiato il pan che si lavora
oggi su l'aje qui; non ha saputo
quanto sudore costi e quale ajuto
dagli altri, per mangiarne: onde veggo ora

quei che lo sanno e sudano agitare
verso la bara piccola il berretto
in saluto: — O figliuol, sii benedetto!
t'ha voluto il Signore risparmiare. —

To Glory

   A death, and the bell does not lament.
Its silvery peal is for glory. A child — is it not?
enters that lofty, white cemetery
with the sea below, the countryside behind it.

   He did not eat the bread they labor for
today, here on the threshing floor. He did not know
how much sweat it cost, and what help
from others, to eat it, and so I watch now

   as those who know and sweat raise
their caps to the little coffin
in farewell: "Oh child, you are blessed!
God only wished to spare you."

Dondolio

Dalla branda, sospesa tra due rami
d'un denso antico olivo saraceno,
gli ultimi ascolto tenui richiami
degli uccelli e il frinire assiduo duro
dei grilli, tra le stoppie, nel sereno
crepuscolo morente. Or sí or no,
  nel lento moto,
gli occhi mi punge, tra il fogliame oscuro,
lo sfavillio d'un piccolo remoto
  astro ch'io non vedrò
forse mai piú, tra tanti altri perduto.

E mentre mi spauro
alle plaghe pensando ultime, donde
la luce di quel mondo a me proviene,
ecco, una fogliolina me l'asconde;
mi scosto, e un' altra volta lo saluto.

Swinging

On the hammock, suspended between
two branches of a thick old saracen
olive tree, I hear the last faint calls
of birds and the raspy chirp
of crickets in the serene dying
of twilight. Now yes, now no,
   in slow motion,
my eyes are struck, through the dark foliage,
by the spark of a tiny distant
   star that I will perhaps
never see again, lost among so many others.
   And now appalled,
thinking of the remotest regions
from where the light of that world comes
to me, a small leaf blocks it out,
I move, and greet it once again.

Compenso

Esausta, muta, sotto l'affocato
baglior, la terra irta di stoppie giace.
Tutto quanto poteva ella ci ha dato.

Ma per chi attese un anno a lavorare
la speranza del premio fu fallace.
Forse perciò sí triste or ella appare?

Se piovve poco, lungo la vernata,
e se ai mandorli il vento portò via
tutti i fiori, e la nebbia attediata

su le biade stagnò, gli olivi oppresse?
Arse pur lei di sete e lei fiorìa
già di quei fior, nudrìa lei quella messe!

Non gliene voglia mal dunque il villano,
e senza tanta rabbia or degli olivi
con la pertica batta i rami piano,

poich'ella in sé li sente mesti e vivi.

RECOMPENSE

   Worn out, mute, under the fiery
glare, the earth bristles with stubble.
She has given us all that she could.

   But for one who labored and waited a year,
the hope of recompense was vain.
Is that, perhaps, why she appears so sad?

If it rained little, the winter was long,
and the wind carried off all the almond
flowers, and the stubborn fog lay upon

   the forage and weighed down the olive trees?
She, too, was parched with thirst, yet already bears
these flowers, nourishes these crops!

   Thus the peasant should not wish her ill,
but strike the olive branches gently
with his pole, and not with anger,

for she feels them in herself, woeful and keen.

Chi resta

Ora che ai cieli dell'autunno mesti
ogni albero, che apparve piú giulivo
del suo bel verde, in disperati gesti
s'irrigidisce e piú non sembra vivo;

 tu con la chioma cinerulea resti
perpetua, sí, grigio stravolto olivo;
d'un vecchio in noi però l'immagin desti;
sempre di gioventú sembrasti privo.

 E se ancor qualche passero s'attarda
su i rami tuoi, smarrito, e con un trillo
breve quest'aure tenta e ascolta e guarda,

 subito lascia le tue fronde austere,
ché a pie' del tronco col suo verso un grillo
par gl'imponga, stizzito, di tacere.

Who Remains

   The trees that seemed so joyful in
their handsome green now stiffen in
the gestures of despair to dreary autumn
skies, and seem alive no longer,

   but you remain, gray crooked olive,
with your changeless, ashen leaves,
yet you bring to mind the image of an aged man
who never seemed to have a youth.

   And if some passing sparrow still
lingers in your boughs, and, with a brief trill,
tests this air, listening and watching,

   he quickly flees your solemn branches
when a cricket at your foot, with its angry song,
seems to demand his silence.

Ritorno

I. La via

Casa romita in mezzo a la natia
campagna, aerea qui, su l'altipiano
d'azzurre argille, a cui sommesso invia
fervor di spume il mare aspro africano,

te sempre vedo, sempre, da lontano,
se penso al punto in cui la vita mia
s'aprí piccola al mondo immenso e vano:
da qui — dico — da qui presi la via.

Da questo sentieruolo tra gli olivi,
di mentastro, di salvie profumato,
m'incamminai pe 'l mondo, ignaro e franco.

E tanto e tanto, o fiorellini schivi
tra l'erma siepe, tanto ho camminato
per ricondurmi a voi, deluso e stanco

II. Rifugio

Il gelso? Non c'è piú. C'è solo il masso
tigrato, ov'io sedea, nascosto, all'ombra.
Vaghi pensieri indefiniti, come. Arcani godimenti,
ansie d'ignota attesa! Eran le foglie
l'ali del ramo? e di volar la brama
non le facea cosí forse brillare?
Cosí gl'incerti desiderii allora
palpitavano in me, quasi senz'ali.

Questo cespuglio di mentastro è forse
quello d'allora? Di fragranza acuta
la mano m'insapora, ed io risento
il sapor di quei dí. Lieto, di corsa,

The Return

1. The Way

   Solitary house in the middle of my native
land, set here, high on the plateau
of blue clay, against which the rough African
sea patiently hurls its seething spume,

   I always see you, always, in the distance,
when I think about the point at which my life,
so tiny, opened on the vast and futile world.
From here, I tell myself, from here I set my course.

   On this narrow path among the olives,
through the wild mint, through perfumed sage,
I went into the world, innocent and artless.

   And much, O timid little blossoms
in the secluded hedge, so much I've wandered,
only to return to you, weary and disappointed.

2. Refuge

   The mulberry tree? Gone. There's only
the veined rock, where I sat, hidden, in its shade.
Vague, nebulous thoughts, faint
as a breath, stirred my childish
soul. Secret pleasures, fears
of the yet unknown! Were leaves
the branch's wings? Didn't longing
to fly make them glitter so?
Thus almost without wings uncertain
desires throbbed in me then.

   Maybe this bush of wild mint
is the same? It scents my hand with a keen
fragrance, and I taste again the flavor
of those days. In joy, I ran here

qui venivo a nascondermi. *Gridavo*
da qui, nascosto, all'eco il nome mio,
e m'incutea misteriosa ambascia
quel sentirmi chiamar da la montagna,
lugubremente. A voce alta pensavo,
con la fidente ingenuità che gli alberi,
i fili d'erba, quelle felci cupe,
l'eriche rosee udissero. Ma forse
non comprendean davvero il mio linguaggio?
Mi carezzava con le foglie il capo
quel gelso, amico e protettor: — «*Bambino,*
ragioni, sí... ma meglio è se tu canti...» —
E i fiori rialzavan le corolle
meravigliati de la mia canzone.
Sovente a lungo ad ajutar qui stavo
le formiche a salir sú sú pe 'l masso;
ma diffidavan quelle, paurose,
de l'ajuto: voleano onestamente
fornir da sé la lunga lor fatica...
Quanto diversi gli uomini...
   Ove sono?
Leggevo. Ecco sul masso il libro aperto.
Il vento passa: sfoglia via di furia
le pagine. L'ha letto... Vanità!

to hide, and hidden, I shouted my name
to the echo, and was struck by a mysterious pang
to hear myself mournfully called from the mountain.
I thought aloud, naively trusting
that the trees, the blades of grass, the dark
ferns and pink heather would hear me.
But perhaps they did not know my language?
The mulberry tree, my friend and protector,
caressed my head with its leaves: "Child,
use reason, yes…but it is better to sing.…"
And flowers raised their corollas
marveling at my song.
Often I stayed for a long time to help.
the ants climb higher and higher on the rock,
but they were mistrustful, afraid of my help:
They wanted in honesty to make
the long effort themselves.…
How different humankind.…
         Where am I?
I was reading. Here on the rock the open book.
The wind rises. It whips the pages
in a fury. It's read them.… Vanity!

ATTESA

Io sono come l'albero che aspetta
la sua stagione e morto intanto pare.
Vien qualche vispa cincia a dimandare:
«Albero, ancora? Bada, è tempo: getta!»
Ma alle cince non dà l'albero retta:
muto ed assorto, rimane a sognare.

Sogna i freschi rampolli, e che tra i rami
verrà per grazia a raccogliere il volo,
ospite prezioso, un rossignuolo.
Piú d'altri uccelli non s'udran richiami.
In ciel, la luna; e magici ricami
d'ombra le frondi stamperan sul suolo.

Sogna e sogna... Ma già forse è passata
la sua stagione, e ad aspettarla sta
l'albero, invano, o forse non verrà
per lui giammai... Se questa, albero, è stata
l'ultima nostra gelida vernata,
che bei sogni la scure abbatterà!

Waiting

   I am like the tree that waits
its season and meanwhile seems dead.
Some breezy titmouse comes to ask:
"Still waiting, tree? Look to it. It's budding time!"
But the tree isn't listening to the birds.
Silent and bemused, he goes on dreaming.

   He dreams new buds, and that among the boughs
he will, by grace of God, receive the flight
of a most precious guest, a nightingale.
More than other birds they're welcomed back.
The moon will fill the sky, and boughs will etch
a magical embroidery of shadow on the ground.

   He dreams and dreams. But maybe his season
has already passed and the tree waits on
in vain, or maybe it will never come
for him.... Tree, if this has been
the last of our icy winters,
what dreams the ax will fell!

FROM

Fuori di Chiave

Offkey

PRELUDIO

Orchestrale

Al violin trillante una sua brava
  sonatina d'amor, con sentimento,
il contrabbasso già da tempo dava
  non so che strano, rauco ammonimento.
Allora io non sapea, che ne la cava
  pancia del mastodontico strumento
si fosse ascosa una mia certa dama
molto magra, senz'occhi, che si chiama?....
           come si chiama?

E invano imperioso, nella destra
  la bacchetta ora stringo: quella mala
signora è del concerto la maestra.
  Da quel suo novo nascondiglio esala
il suo frigido fiato nell'orchestra
  sale di tono ogni strumento o cala,
le corde si rilassano, gli ottoni
s'arrochiscono o mandan certi suoni....
           Dio le perdoni!

M'arrabbio, grido, spezzo la bacchetta,
  balzo in piedi, m'ajuto con la mano.
La sonata è patetica; dian retta
  i violini: piano, piano, piano...
Ma che piano! Di là, la maladetta,
  sforza il tempo, rovescia l'uragano!
Da otto nove a due quarti, a otto sei...
  Vi prego di pigliarvela con Lei,
           signori miei.

Di partenza

Tele di ragno lavorate a maglia
finissima, le vele (o mie discrete
    speranze liete!):

PRELUDE

Orchestral

To the violin trilling its heartfelt
  song of love, the contrabass
has for some time been giving
  a sort of strange, hoarse admonition.
Now I don't know if in the hollow
  belly of the mammoth instrument
may be concealed a certain woman of mine,
very thin, without eyes, whose name is…
                    what is her name?

And vainly imperious, I clutch the baton
  in my right hand. That wicked lady
now conducts the concert.
  From her new hiding place, her icy breath
spreads into the orchestra;
  the sound of every instrument rises or falls,
the strings grow slack, the brass
  are hoarse or send out certain sounds…
                    God forgive them!

I am furious, cry out, break the baton,
  leap to my feet, do my best with my hand.
The sonata is pathetic. The violins listen,
  softly, softly, softly.… But what softly!
From the contrabass the accursed lady
  forces the tempo, unleashes a hurricane!
From *eight nine* to *two four*, to *eight six*…
  I beg you to take her with you when you go,
                  gentlemen.…

Of Departure

Spider webs worked in the finest
stitch, the sails (of my modest
      hopes of happiness!);

l'albero, un grosso e lungo fil di paglia,
che simboleggia il novello ideale
o la fede novella; il sartiame
   fatto di trame
di sentimenti, tutto a nodi e a scale;
lo scafo costruito di gusciaglia:
io parto, amici: eccomi pronto. E butto,
senza stare a pensar se poi m'occorra,
   ogni zavorra
di fede antica ed ogni inganno, tutto.
Senza bussola e senza àncora vo.
Dove? Imprendo un viaggio di scoperta.
   La mèta e incerta.
Ma, chi sa! Forse il regno troverò
che da tant'anni cerco senza frutto.

So che, lasciando questo porto, in preda
la nave mia cadrà di tutti i venti
   più violenti;
ed avverrà che forse più non veda,
né da vicin né da lontano, alcuna
spiaggia, né scorga alcun remoto faro.
   Per quanto amaro
però mi sia, convien che la fortuna
tenti e alla smania che mi spinge, io ceda.

Duolmi che se m'avvenga di trovare
alfine il regno, piú non possa io poi
   tornare a voi;
che folle è il vento: traccia vie sul mare
e le cancella poi, come gli frulla.
Di partir senza bussola m'è forza;
   piú della scorza
a cui m'affido peserebbe, e a nulla
poi gioverebbe pe 'l mio navigare.

the mast, a thick and lengthy blade of straw
that symbolizes the new ideal
or the new faith; the shrouds
  made of the warp
of feelings more and more knotted;
the hull built of shells;
I leave, friends, here I am, ready. And I throw away
without stopping to think if I will need it later,
  every ballast
of ancient faith and every lie, all.
Without compass and without anchor I go.
Where? I begin a voyage of discovery.
  The goal is uncertain.
But who knows! Perhaps I will find the kingdom
that I have been seeking so many years without success.

I know that, leaving this port, my boat
will be prey to all the most
  violent winds;
and it will so happen perhaps that I will not see,
either from near or far off, any beach,
nor catch sight of any distant beacon.
  Nevertheless, however bitter
it is for me, it is better that I test
fortune and submit to the craving that drives me on.

It grieves me that if I happen to find
the kingdom at last, I won't be able then
  to return to you,
for the wind is mad: it traces paths on the sea
and then cancels them as it lashes them.
I am compelled to leave without a compass.
  More than the surface
in which I put my faith would it weigh on me. Then
it would be no use to me in my voyage.

INGRESSO

All'ingresso della vita,
timoroso, m'affacciai
da una porta semichiusa.
Vi picchiai sú con due dita,
poi con garbo dimandai:
— «È permesso? Chiedo scusa...
Entro o no?...» — Silenzio.
Spingo allor, pian pian, la porta.
Bujo pesto. Ne sorrido;
ma agghiacciar dentro mi sento.
— «Che la vita sia già morta?» —
Vo tentoni; inciampo; un grido
mi riempie di spavento:
— «Non ci vedi? Canchero!» —
Chi un fiammifero ora sfrega
in quel bujo alla parete?
Ecco lume alfine. Vedo
una vecchia, sconcia strega
chi mi spia; poi fa: — «Chi siete?»
— «Ecco, — le rispondo, — chiedo
scusa dell'incomodo...
Io son un che arriva adesso.
Sarà tardi? Nel viaggio
ho la via forse smarrita...
Ma — potendo — col permesso,
lesto lesto, di passagio,
visitar vorrei la vita.
Me ne vado subito...» —

— «Ah, tu pur, tu pur d'entrare
nella vita hai voglia? Sciocco!
Che t'aspetti? dimmi un po'...
Non hai dunque altro da fare?» —
Sto a guardar come un alloco

ENTRANCE

At the entrance to life,
anxious, I peered through
a half-opened door.
I knocked with two fingers,
then politely inquired…
"May I? Excuse me
   Can I come in or not?…" Silence.

Then very slowly, I nudge the door.
Utter darkness. I grin,
but ice is what I feel inside.
"Can life be dead already?"
I grope ahead, stumble. A scream
terrifies me:
   "Can't you see? You pest!"

Who now strikes a match on
the wall in this darkness?
There's some light at last. I see
a hag, a filthy witch,
squinting at me. "Who are you?" she asks.
"Sorry," I answer, "I beg your pardon
   for disturbing you…

"I'm just arriving.
Am I late? I may have
gotten lost along the way.…
But, if I can, if you'll let me,
quickly, just in passing,
take a look at life,
   I'll leave in no time.…"

"So, even the likes of you
wants to give life a try? You idiot!
What do you expect? Tell me.…
Haven't you anything better to do?"
Like a dolt I look around

e rispondo: — «Ma... non so...
non so nulla... proprio...» —
— «Eh, si vede! — allor soggiunge
la stregaccia. — Piglia a caso
la tua sorte, e ben t'occorra!
Pria d'entrare, ognun che giunge,
si fornisce in questo vaso
d'un malanno per zavorra.
 Sai l'antica storia
di Promèteo e di Pandora?
Sú, sú, prendi: il vaso è qui.
Io Pandora son; vecchiaja
maledetta! vivo ancora,
e ridotta son cosí
a far qui da portinaja.
 Basta. Hai preso? Sbrigati!» —

Affondai la man tremante
in quel cavo enorme, oscuro,
e la sorte mia pescai;
poscia entrai... Ne ho viste tante,
che oramai piú non mi curo
di saper qual male mai
 rechi la mia tessera.

and answer: "But…I don't know…
　　don't know anything…really.…"

"So I see!" Then the old witch
adds: "Pick out your fate
by chance, and hope for the best!
Before they enter, all who come here
draw an affliction as ballast
from this bowl. Do you know
　　the ancient tale

of Prometheus and Pandora?
Go on, go on, take one. Here's the bowl.
I'm Pandora, cursed
with age! Still alive,
brought low like this,
to serve as doorkeeper here.
　　Enough! Have you chosen? Hurry up!"

I thrust my trembling hand
into that huge, dark opening
and drew my fate, then entered.…
By now I've seen so many evils
that I don't care to know
which one it was
　　my ticket brought me.

LA MÈTA

I

Una mèta! una mèta! Ma sul ramo
forse da sé la pània in che s'invesca
s'apparecchia l'uccello? o il pesce all'amo
   l'esca?

E deve l'uom da sé piantarsi il palo,
sospendervi una fune a un qualche chiodo,
creder quel palo
            gloria
            donna
            fortuna
        o non so ch'altro scialo,
perché — conscio — s'impicchi in qualche modo?

II

Mettiti a camminare,
va' dove il piè ti porta,
piglia la via piú corta
e piú non dimandare.

Andar dove che sia,
nel dubbio della sorte,
andar verso la morte
per un'ignota via:

ecco il destino. E dunque
fa' quel che far si deve.
Procura che sia breve.
Tanto, è lo stesso ovunque.

The Goal

1

A goal! a goal! But may not the bird
on the branch itself prepare the lime
in which it's caught? Or the fish the bait
    on the hook?

And should man himself drive in a stake,
nail a rope to it,
and swear that it is
    glory
    woman
    fortune
    or who knows what other extravagance,
so that, quite consciously, he somehow hangs himself?

2

Start walking,
go where your feet take you,
pick the shortest way,
ask nothing more.

To make one's way
unsure of fate,
to go toward death
by an unknown path,

that's destiny. And so,
do what must be done.
Try to make it brief.
Besides, it's everywhere the same.

Il pianeta

I

Gira, gira…Nello spazio
tante trottole. Ci scherza
Dio. Talvolta con la trottola
di man sfuggegli la ferza,

ed in cielo allor si vedono
le comete… — O savio antico,
teco or piú non posso io credere
che la terra l'ombelico

sia del mondo e che s'aggirino
sole ed astri a lei d'attorno
per offrirle uno spettacolo
e far lume notte e giorno.

Se sapessi con che fervido
indefesso acuto zelo
ci siam messi noi medesimi
a scoprirci atomi in cielo!

II

Ma la Terra, se non bella,
via, non c'è poi tanto male:
dican pure ch'è una stella
d'infim'ordine; che vale?

C'è bei monti, c'è ubertosi
pani, e poi ci sono mari,
Se vogliamo, spaziosi…
Forse i viveri son cari.

Città belle, ve ne sono:
per esempio, dove metti
Roma? Vino e vitto buono;
buone donne; buoni letti…

The Planet

1

Spinning, spinning…so many tops
spinning in space. God toys
with them. Sometimes the string slips
and the top flies from his hand,

and then in the heavens comets
are seen.… O wise ancient
with you I can no longer believe
that the Earth may be the navel

of the cosmos and that the sun
and stars turn around her
to offer her a spectacle
and illumine night and day.

If you knew with what fervid,
tireless and unflinching zeal
we have applied ourselves
to discover that we are atoms in the sky!

2

But the Earth, if not beautiful,
is not so bad after all,
and they say, too, it's a star
of the lowest rank — so what?

There are splendid mountains and rich
plains, and then there are oceans,
spacious, we might say.…
Maybe the cost of living is high.

There are beautiful cities:
for example, what about
Rome? Wine and good food,
good women, good beds.…

Piú poeti in belli squarci
n'han già reso grazie a Dio.
Ma che siam venuti a farci?
Tu lo sai? No? Neppur io.

III

Non siam fatti per capire
tutto in prima. Pazienza!
Dovrem pure un dí morire.
La ragion dell'esistenza

la sapremo, forse, dopo.
E che fare intanto? Attendere
alla vita e, a breve scopo,
per non stare in ozio, prendere

una cosa pur che sia,
seria or vana, importa poco:
quel che importa é che si dia
importanza al proprio gioco.

Giacché stolto é l'uom che vuole
ragionar le cose arcane,
fabbricando di parole
vane, leggi ancor piú vane.

Di sentenze n'ho sentite
d'ogni conio: dolci e amare;
ma, tra loro, tutte in lite:
un continuo mareggiare.

Sieno vere queste or quelle,
forse é meglio viver solo
per amar le donne belle…—
ma ne vien qualche figliuolo.

Many poets in beautiful verses
have already thanked God for them.
But what have we come here to do?
Do you know? No? Nor do I.

3

We are not made to understand
everything at once. Patience!
Someday, too, we'll have to die.
Maybe afterward we'll know

the reason of existence.
And meantime, what to do? Attend
to life and, in the short run,
not be idle, choose

one thing, whatever it may be,
serious or vain, it doesn't matter.
What matters is to give
importance to one's game.

Since the man's a fool who wants
to reason on things mysterious,
fabricating laws from futile words
is the most futile thing of all.

I've heard opinions
of every stamp, sweet and bitter,
but all conflict with all the others
in continual upheaval.

Be these true or those,
perhaps it's better just to live
for the love of pretty women....
But then a child comes of it.

IV

Facciam conto una vettura
questa nostra Terra sia,
sempre in giro, alla ventura,
su cui far dobbiam la via.

Postiglione, il vecchio Tempo;
passager' precarii, noi:
forse, in prima, è passatempo;
poi, col tempo, ti ci annoj.

Giornalmente il vetturale
vien lo scotto a dimandare:
c'è chi scende, c'è chi sale,
ma ciascun deve pagare.

E il viaggio costa assai,
e si sta scomodi bene;
si va sempre innanzi e mai
a destin non si perviene.

Io, per me, forse v'ascesi
troppo tardi, e ci sto male.
Tutti i posti erano presi:
seggo su l'imperiale.

Stelle e nuvole pe 'l cielo
di guardar solo m'è dato:
m'è nell'ossa entrato il gelo
e sternuti alzo al creato.

Graziosi i venticelli
scherzan su la testa mia
e gl'inganni ed i capelli
tutti, aimè, mi portan via.

D'aspettar cosí mi resta,
paziente passeggere,
ch'abbia fine per me questa
strana gita di piacere.

4

Let's imagine that our Earth
is a coach, always in motion,
driven by chance,
on which we have to make our way.

Old Time is the postilion,
nervous passengers, we.
Perhaps at first it's a joyride,
then, with time, you get bored.

Every day the coachman
comes to collect the fare.
Some get on, some get off,
but everyone must pay.

And the trip costs quite a lot,
and one doesn't ride in comfort.
You keep going on forever
and never arrive anywhere.

As for me, perhaps I came aboard
too late, and I'm very ill at ease.
All the seats were taken
so I sit outside on top.

Stars and clouds in the sky
are all I have to look at.
The chill has reached my bones,
and I send the world my sneezes.

The breezes gracefully
play about my head,
and take away, alas, all
my illusions and my hair.

All that's left me is to wait,
a patient passenger,
until this strange pleasure trip
brings me to my end.

Credo

Tengo a vantarmi solo d'una cosa,
cioè:
d'aver per tempo appreso che si sente
pure una gioja, ancora a molti ascosa,
nel non chieder perché
di niente
né a Dio nostro signore, né alla sposa
di Dio, madre Natura, né alla gente;
e nel lasciar che i cosí detti scaltri
non prestin essi fede alla bugia
che altri
dal nostro stesso dimandar sovente
a dir costretto sia.

Se Dio mi vuol far credere ch'Egli è
dovunque
e che
veglia su tutti, e dunque
pure su me;
ch'Egli d'una giustizia è dispensiere
la qual col nostro metro
non si misura né intender ci è dato,
dovrò dargli per questo dispiacere?
gli crederò:
il mondo, bene o male, ha camminato,
almeno un po';
Egli non sa mutar l'antico andare,
povero Vecchio, ed è rimasto indietro.
Ma il mal non lo so fare,
e alle labbra, che chiacchieran da mane
a sera,
che costa, alla fin fine, una preghiera?
Io rimango credente, ei Dio rimane.

Chi d'inventar si piaccia
stranissime avventure

CREED

I can boast of one thing only,
which is:
to have learned early on the joy
one feels, still hidden from many,
in not asking the why
of anything,
not of God our Lord, nor the bride
of God, Mother Nature, nor of people,
and letting those accounted wise
put their faith in the lie
that another,
by our own constant questioning,
is forced to tell.

If God wishes me to believe that He is
everywhere,
and that
He watches over everyone, and therefore
over me as well,
that He metes out a justice
we can't measure with our yardstick or comprehend,
should I offend Him just for that?
I will believe Him.
The world, for better or worse, has gone
its way at least a little while.
He cannot change its ancient rhythm,
poor Old Fellow, and now is left behind.
But I've no wish to trouble Him,
and to lips that babble from dawn
to dark,
how much does a prayer cost, after all?
I remain a believer, He remains God.

Whoever wants to conjure up
fantastic deeds

e trovar brami chi fede gli presti,
venga da me, venga e le narri pure;
di stupor, d'ira o di duol, com'ei vuole,
vedrà tosto atteggiarsi la mia faccia,
seguendo le parole
e i gesti.
Poco mi costerà farlo felice.
E non m'importa s'egli poi balordo
mi dice:
so d'essere la rete ed egli il tordo.

and yearns for others to have faith in him,
let him come to me, come and tell me all,
he will see reflected in my face
the wonder, rage, or sadness he desires,
agreeing with his words
and gestures.
It will cost me little enough to make him happy.
And then who cares if he considers me
a fool.
I know that I'm the snare and he the thrush.

Il tesoro

Ricco jeri, oggi povero. E non so
   com'ita se ne sia tanta ricchezza.
   Non del tesor perduto è l'amarezza;
ma il non saper come perduto io l'ho.

Nessun piacer, nessuna gioja, aimè,
   la cui memoria avrebbe almen potuto
   consolar la miseria e il viver muto,
o dello stato mio dirmi il perché.

Come dunque ridotto mi son qui?
   Con la ricchezza mia potea far tanto,
   e nulla ho fatto, e son povero intanto...
L'ho sperduta in ispiccioli, cosí...

Non l'opera che dia lustro a un'età,
   né la gioja ch'empir possa una vita.
   Dunque tanta ricchezza m'è servita
per comperarmi questa povertà.

Wealth

Rich yesterday, today poor. And I don't know
   where all that wealth has gone.
   The bitterness is not for riches lost,
but not knowing how I lost them.

Not one pleasure, not one joy, alas,
   that could at least in memory console
   me for poverty and a mute life,
or give me the reason for my state.

How, then, was I so reduced?
   With my wealth I could have done so much,
   and have done nothing, and am poor besides....
I wasted it on trivial things, just so....

Not the work that gives glory to an age,
   nor the joy that can fulfill a life.
   So all my treasure has served
to buy me this poverty.

Vecchio avviso

Quand'ero al Reno... O amici miei Renani
dal franco, onesto viso!
Cercando tra le carte, un vecchio avviso
a stampa m'è venuto tra le mani:

    NEL VIALE DEI PIOPPI OGGI ALL'APERTO
    POCO DOPO LE TRE
    OFFRONO AGLI AVVENTORI DEL CAFFÈ
    GLI USSERI TROMBETTIERI UN GRAN CONCERTO.

Parean giganti degli antichi miti.
Trenta. E dentro ai polmoni
tutto il vento del nord. Ai loro tuoni
vedevo i pioppi tremare atterriti,

e le foglie cader come farfalle
morte, e uccelli cadere,
spennati questi dalle trombe fiere
e quelle fatte qual per verno gialle.

Guardavo il ciel pensando: — «Or or si squarcia!
Morranno gli avventori?» —
Ma che! Beati. Giú birra e liquori,
e col canto seguivano la marcia.

Poi, come presi da improvvisa insania,
  in piedi, coi bicchieri
levati verso i trenta trombettieri,
tre volte urlaron: — «Viva la Germania!» —

An Old Notice

When I was on the Rhine — O my Rhenish friends
   with your frank, your honest faces! —
as I was looking through my papers, an old printed
notice came to hand:

> TODAY OUTDOORS ON THE AVENUE OF POPLARS
> A LITTLE AFTER THREE
> A GRAND CONCERT WILL BE PRESENTED TO PATRONS
> OF THIS CAFÉ BY THE HUSSAR TRUMPETERS.

They looked like giants from the ancient myths.
   Thirty of them. And in their lungs
were all the northern winds. I saw the poplars
tremble, frightened at their thunderous blasts,

and the leaves fell like dead butterflies,
   turned yellow as if by winter,
and the birds fell, plucked clean
by the sound of those heroic horns.

I stared at the sky and thought, "Now it will split!
   Will all the patrons die?"
Hardly! They're in bliss. Down go beer and booze,
and they follow the march with a song.

Then, as if they had suddenly gone mad,
   they're on their feet. With glasses
lifted to the thirty trumpeters,
they shout three times: "Long live Germany!"

Melbthal

I

Quella giubbetta a maglia
come le stava bene!
e, ornato di vermene,
quel gran cappel di paglia.

D'un subito s'accorse
che mi piaceva assai:
rise negli occhi gaj
ed il labbro si morse.

— «Vengo sú al bosco a un patto, —
poi disse, — e bada tu!
che d'amore, lassú,
noi non si parli affatto.»

— Else! — esclamai. Ma lesta
sui labbri ella una mano
mi pose; io, piano piano,
gliela baciai. La testa

scosse. — «Cominci male!...
Se fai cosí...Sú, andiamo.
Ricordati: io non t'amo
piú — passato il viale.»

II

Il bosco parea fatto
per perderci ambidue.
Ma su le labbra sue
leggevo ancora il patto.

Tutti, tutti gli uccelli
m'incitavan dai rami:
«Dille, dille che l'ami!
Baciale gli occhi belli!»

Melbthal

1

That knitted jacket —
how well it became her!
And that big straw hat
adorned with verbena.

She saw at once
how much I liked her.
Her gay eyes laughed,
and she bit her lip.

"I'll come to the woods," she said,
"on one condition, and listen
carefully, you! That we'll not speak
a word of love there."

"Else!" I cried. But she laid
a hand lightly over my
mouth. Softly, softly, I
kissed it. She shook

her head. "You're starting badly!...
If you act like that.... Come, let's go.
Remember, I don't love you
any more — once we cross the road."

2

The woods seemed made
for us to lose ourselves.
But on her lips
I still read the condition.

All the birds
urged me from the branches:
"Tell her, tell her that you love her!
Kiss her lovely eyes!"

E, vedendo ogni fiore
il mio cipiglio fosco:
«Perché venire al bosco,
se non fate all'amore?»

E ov'era piú raccolta
l'ombra, volgeansi gli occhi:
«Oh ben voi siete sciocchi!
Qui l'erba è molle a folta...»

E in basso ecco garrire
la Melb, il ruscel tenue:
«Oh quante coppie ingenue
qui vengonsi a scaltrire!»

III

Ella ciarlava molto,
senza guardarmi, e certo
sentia col senso esperto
ch'io non le davo ascolto.

Dicea: — «La Melb ha foce
nel Reno, sai? Di fronte
hai di Venere il monte
e il monte della Croce.

Nessun dei due t'adeschi!
Qua il fuoco e lì la cenere:
la Croce accanto a Venere.
Filosofi, i Tedeschi!»

S'accorse o non s'accorse
che, tra i discorsi vani,
s'eran le nostre mani
cercate e avvinte? Forse.

Ché cominciò man mano
a tremarle la voce.
— E la Melb, dunque, ha foce
nel Reno? Oh caso strano... —

And all the flowers seeing
my sullen frown:
"Why come into the woods,
if you're not making love?"

And turning their eyes to where
the shade was densely gathered:
"Oh what utter fools you are!
Here the grass is soft and thick.…"

And down below, the Melb's
thin stream murmured to us:
"Oh how many innocent couples
come here to grow more wise!"

3

She chattered a lot,
her eyes averted, and surely
she knew, with her keen sense,
that I was hardly listening.

She said: "Do you know the Melb
runs into the Rhine? Opposite
you see the mountain of Venus
and the mountain of the Cross.

Neither is very inviting!
Here the fire and there the ashes,
the Cross alongside Venus.
Philosophers, the Germans!"

Did she or did she not take note,
while she was rattling on,
that our hands had sought
each other, and clasped? Perhaps.

Gradually her voice
began to tremble.
"So the Melb, then, runs into
the Rhine? How strange.…"

— «Sí, sí, proprio laggiú,
dopo i molini, a manca...
Oh Dio, sono già stanca.
Di', non sei stanco tu?»

*Sedemmo all'ombra. Ah, il patto
fu mantenuto appieno.
D'amor, sen contro seno,
noi non parlammo affatto.*

"Yes, yes, just over there,
beyond the windmills, on the left....
O God, I'm tired already.
Aren't you tired as well?"

We sat down in the shade. Ah,
the condition was fully met.
Of love, breast to breast,
not a word was said.

Primavera dei terrazzi

La mia vicina, sul mattin d'aprile,
compresa ancora del tepor del letto,
esce al terrazzo, e al sol primaverile
spiega i tesori del ricolmo petto.
Ella ha piú grazia, la vicina, in quella
acconciatura che le cangia aspetto:
un camicino bianco e una gonnella
di panno lano oscura. La saluto
dal mio poggiolo dirimpetto, ed ella,
lieve inchinando il capo riccioluto,
mi risponde; poi viene al pilastrino,
su cui ride snasato un fauno arguto,
e dice: — «Come mai, caro vicino?
siete voi? sogno ancora? o com'è andata?
qual gallo v'ha cantato il mattutino?» —

Cosí, tra i fior, su la balaustrata,
dei vasi ben disposti e con amore
coltivati da lei lungo l'annata,
un grande anch'ella pare e vivo fiore;
anzi, lei sola, un fiore. A quel giardino,
giro giro, che calci di gran cuore
darei! parmi ogni vaso un cervellino
di moderno romantico poeta
che levi dal suo fango un inno fino
tra il cessin le pillaccole e la creta
per dir che piú non ama e piú non spera
alla stagion che tutto il mondo allieta.
Oh dei terrazzi magra primavera,
sciocca di nuove rime fioritura!
Mi duol che voi, maestra giardiniera,
ve ne prendiate cosí assidua cura.
Codesti fiori dall'olezzo ingrato
non vi sembrano sforzi di natura?
Due tartarughe, intanto, senza fiato,
s'inseguono sui pie' sbiechi, in amore,

SPRINGTIME ON THE TERRACES

My neighbor, on an April morning,
still flushed with the warmth of bed,
steps out on her terrace and opens to the spring sun
the riches of her overflowing bosom.
She has much charm, the neighbor, in that
attire which changes her appearance:
a white bodice and a skirt
of dark wool cloth. I greet her
from my balcony opposite, and she,
with a slight nod of her curly head,
responds, then she comes to the column
on which there laughs a noseless, witty faun,
and says: "Can it be, dear neighbor?
Is it you? Do I still dream? How has it happened?
What cock has sung the matins to you?"

Thus, among the flowers on the balustrade,
the well-placed pots she has lovingly
cultivated all year long,
she, too, appears a large and brilliant flower,
or rather, she alone is a flower. In that garden
I'd go round and round, and what swift kicks
I'd give! I seem to see in every pot the tiny head
of a modern romantic poet,
who raises from his mud a delicate hymn
amid manure, the potting soil, and clay,
to say he loves no more and hopes no more
in the season when all the world rejoices.
Oh meagre spring of terraces,
foolish with the flowering of new rhymes!
It saddens me that you, the mistress of the garden,
take such assiduous care of them.
These flowers with their disagreeable smell,
don't they seem miscarriages of nature?
Meanwhile two turtles, out of breath,
pursue each other in love, their splayed feet

raspando il piano d'asfalto bruciato.
Cara vicina, fatemi il favore
di rivoltarle su la scaglia al sole:
non hanno alcun riguardo, alcun pudore,
brutte rocciose sceme bestiole;
sono lí lí per fare atto villano,
mentre che noi facciam solo parole:

le vedremo armeggiar nel vuoto, invano.

clawing at the hot asphalt pavement.
Dear neighbor, do me a favor
and turn them on their backs in the sun;
they lack all decency, all shame,
ugly, hard, stupid little beasts,
they're just about to do a boorish act,
while we make only words.

We'll watch them vainly thrashing in the air.

L'OCCHIO PER LA MORTE

Sono stato a veder l'amico morto.
Sta benone. Men brutto (ah, brutto egli era,
povero amico!): e quel pallor di cera
e la calma in cui sta da savio assorto,
gli dànno or l'aria mesta e tollerante,
che si sforzò d'avere in vita, e certo
non ebbe. Intanto, che peccato! aperto
gli è rimasto quell'occhio, che in costante
studio lo tenne: or possiam dirlo, credo:
l'occhio di vetro. Orrendo, nella faccia
spenta, quel guardo fiso, di minaccia...
Quell'occhio par che dica ora: — «Io ci vedo!»

An Eye for Death

I've been to see our friend who died.
He's fine. Less ugly (oh, he was ugly,
our poor friend!), and that waxy pallor
and the sage's calm in which he rests,
engrossed in thought, give him the sad
and tolerant air he strove for in his life,
and surely never had. Meanwhile, what a pity!
The eye remains wide open that was always
on his mind. We can say it now, I think,
the glass eye. Horrific on the lifeless
face, that rigid stare of menace....
The eye now seems to say, "I see you all!"

Onorio

Perché sí bello han fatto il campanile
                cinquecent'anni fa?
Perché, venendo alla nostra città,
gl'Inglesi ne ammirassero lo stile.

E d'opra fina è tutto ornato il bronzo
                delle sette campane,
onde, fino alle case piú lontane,
quando han sonato, si propaga il ronzo.

Le suona uno scaccino gobbo, guercio,
                saltabellante; Onorio,
che con l'anime pie del purgatorio
è — le beghine dicono — in commercio.

Piangono gli occhi e dal cuore contrito
                si leva la preghiera
quando le suona Onorio innanzi sera,
sfruconandosi il naso con un dito.

Ah, Onorio, tu non sai che voglia dire
                il suon d'una campana!
Della città tumultua qua la vana
vita, fermenta l'odio e scoppian ire,

scoppian rampogne e risa e pianti; sú
                mesta la fede Iddio
chiama in ajuto, invoca requie e oblio!
E pensar che la fune in man l'hai tu...

Onorio

Why was the bell tower so beautifully made
                five hundred years ago,
so that the English tourists, coming to
our city, wonder at its style?

So finely worked and embellished is the bronze
                of the seven bells
that, when they've rung out, the tolling spreads
as far as the farthest houses.

A squint-eyed, limping, hunchbacked
                sexton rings them:
Onorio, who, as the Beguines tell it,
has dealings with the pious souls in Purgatory.

Eyes fill with tears and prayer rises
                from the contrite heart,
when Onorio rings the bells at dusk,
picking his nose with a finger.

Ah, Onorio, you can't know what it means,
                the tolling of a bell!
The vain life of the city runs riot here,
hatred ferments and rage bursts out,

and reproaches, and laughter, and tears;
                up there faith sadly appeals
to the Lord for help, for peace and oblivion!
And to think it's your hand that holds the rope....

Stormo

Pace dei campi, requie della morte.
Qua presso, in cima al poggio, è il cimitero.
Olivi in giro; e veglia su le porte
un drappel di cipressi ispido, nero.

O morti, il bujo della vostra sorte,
mi fa sembrar comprese del pensiero
mio stesso queste frondi aspre, contorte,
e l'aria intorno, piena di mistero.

Mi volgo a ogni romor lieve che fanno
gl'insetti e i fili d'erba a quando a quando,
avviluppati in quest'arcana noja.

Ma ecco, a un tratto, squilla come un bando:
sono gridi d'uccelli ebbri di gioja,
che né di voi, né della morte sanno.

Flight of Birds

Peace in the fields, the stillness of death.
Nearby, at the hillock's crest, the cemetery lies.
Olive trees all around, and keeping vigil at the gate
a troop of black and shaggy cypresses.

O dead, the darkness of your fate
makes it seem as if these rough, contorted
boughs are filled with my own thoughts,
and the air around is full of mystery.

I turn at every little sound that now and then
the insects make, and the blades of grass,
wrapped in this arcane tedium.

But suddenly, shrill as a proclamation:
the cries of birds made drunk with joy,
who know neither you nor death.

Sempre bestia

Senza far nulla, un leone è leone:
e un pover'uom dev'affrontar la morte
per avere l'onor del paragone
con quella bestia, senza stento, forte.

D'alti pensieri l'anima infelice
nutrite, sí che s'alzi a eccelse mète.
Un gran premio v'aspetta. Vi si dice
che veramente un'aquila voi siete.

Sciogliete in soavissima armonia
il vostro chiuso intenso ardente duolo,
fatene una sublime poesia,
e vi diran che siete un rosignuolo.

Ma dunque per non essere una bestia
che dovrebbe far l'uomo? non far niente?
non pigliarsi ne affanno ne molestia?
E ciuco allora gli dirà la gente.

Chiú

Che hai fatto? Dimmi, forse perché
sei nato gufo, piangi cosí?
credi forse che peggio di te
non ci sian bestie, gufo? Ma sí,
ce n'è, ce n'è!
Io ne conosco,
non lì nel bosco —
tante ce n'è!

Always an Animal

Without doing a thing, a lion is a lion,
and a mere man has to confront death
to have the honor of being likened
to that beast, so effortlessly strong.

You nourish an unhappy soul with noble thoughts
so it will rise to lofty ends.
A great reward awaits you. You'll be told
you really are an eagle.

Pour out in sweetest melody
your secret, burning, most impassioned grief.
Make of it a sublime poem,
and they will say you are a nightingale.

What then must a man do in order
not to become an animal? Do nothing?
Avoid what's difficult or troublesome?
Then people will call him ass.

To-whoo

What have you done? Tell me, perhaps because
you were born an owl you mourn so?
Perhaps you think there are no creatures
worse than you, owl? But yes,
there are, there are!
I know some,
not here in the woods —
there are many!

Meriggio

Segano l'afa le cicale. Acuto,
sottile e lamentoso, ad ora ad ora,
requie uno strido di pispola implora
qua, dalla macchia cedua, ov'io seduto
mi sto su un ceppo, e l'ombra mi ristora.

Calan ne l'ombra a un fil de la seguace
lor bava appesi, giú da cima, i ragni.
O pispola mia dolce, che ti lagni
de lo stridor de le cicale, pace
non han neppur gl'insetti, tra i castagni.

Ci sono i ragni! E ci son le formiche
anche per me... Ce n'ho già tante addosso
Sú entratemi pe 'l naso, fino all'osso,
portatevi, formiche, al vostro fosso.

Se Dio v'aiuta, finita l'estate,
sentirete che gusto! Entrate, entrate...

Guardando il mare

E sei vivo anche tu, come son io:
tu per molto, io per poco, e ne son lieto.
Ma ti vedo e ti penso, io; tu non vedi
e non pensi, beato! Fino ai piedi
vieni con un sommesso fragorío
a stendermi le spume, mansueto.

Come un mercante di merletti... Bravo!
Uno ne stendi, e tosto lo ritrai,
ed ecco un altro, e un altro ancora... Scempio
fai cosí della tua grandezza, ignavo?
Tenta, prova altri scherzi... non ne sai?
Ma ingójati la terra, per esempio!

High Noon

Cicadas pierce the sultry air. High-pitched,
keen, and plaintive, a strident pipit's cry,
from time to time, begs for peace,
here in the underbrush of the copse where I sit
on a stump, the shade restoring me.

In the shade, spiders drop from the treetops,
hanging by the thread of their trailing spittle.
O my sweet pipit complaining
of the cicadas' shrillness, not even
the insects find peace among the chestnut trees.

There are the spiders. And there are ants also
for me.… I feel them crawling on me now!
Come, enter my nose, as deep as the bone,
my dears, and the brain, reduced to crumbs,
bear it away, ants, into your nest.

With God's help, summer passed,
you will enjoy such a feast! Come in, come in.…

Looking at the Sea

So you're alive also, as am I,
you for ages, I briefly, and glad of it.
But I see you and think of you. You don't
see or think, lucky devil! You come
up to my feet with muffled roar,
and graze me gently with your foam.

Like a merchant showing lace.… How fine!
You hold a sample out, then snatch it back,
then another, and another.… Is that the way
you bring ruin with your vastness, indolent one?
Try some other tricks…or have you none?
For instance, swallow the earth!

Convegno

I

Per le città, nostre o d'oltralpe, in ogni
luogo, ov'ho fatto alcun tempo dimora,
io vedo un altro me, com'ero allora,
il qual lieto s'aggira entro a quei sogni,
che suoi soltanto e non pur miei son ora.

Né verun d'essi sa, che piú ne sia
di me. Qua vive o là, chiuso ciascuno
nel proprio tempo. Oltre non vede. E uno
si ferma, or ecco, a sera, in una via
di Como, e guarda in sú, se un viso bruno...

Ahi, quella bruna — egli no 'l sa — maestra
ora è di vizii e di sé locandiera...
Ma come può saperlo, se ogni sera
davvero ancor s'affaccia alla finestra
ella, e d'amor gli parla ed è sincera?

L'altro, eccolo in Germania, a Bonn sul Reno,
sotto un cappello di castoro, enorme:
magro egro smunto: non mangia, non dorme;
studia sul serio (o cosí crede almeno)
del linguaggio le origini e le forme.

Studia, ma... è notte: brontola il camino;
fuori, la neve lenta eterna fiocca:
pian l'uscio s'apre e, un dito su la bocca,
entra scalza Jenny... Libro latino,
di ravvivare il fuoco ora ti tocca!

Oh, chi a Palermo incontrasse per caso
quell'altro me, che della vita mia
la stagione piú bella tuttavia
colà si gode, sgombro e ancor non raso
il mento, alato il cor di poesia,

A Meeting

1

In the cities where I sometime lived,
both ours or those beyond the Alps,
I see another me as I was then,
who gladly wanders in those dreams
that now are only his and mine no more.

None of them knows what has become
of me. Each lives here or there, sealed off
in his own time. He cannot see beyond. And one
pauses — there he is now — at dusk, on a street
in Como, and he glances up, if a dark face....

Ah, that dark one! — he doesn't know it —
is mistress of vices now, and herself for sale....
But how can he know, if every evening
she still leans from her window
and talks to him of love and is sincere?

Another, there he is in Germany, in Bonn
on Rhine, under an enormous beaver hat.
Thin and sickly pale, he neither eats nor sleeps.
A fervent student (or so he thinks, at least)
of the forms and origins of language.

He studies but…it's night, the fireplace mutters.
Outside the slow, eternal snow is falling.
softly the door is opened, and a finger on her lips,
Jenny enters barefoot.... Latin book,
it's up to you to start the fire again!

Oh, whoever chanced to meet, when in Palermo,
that other me who still delights there
in the sweetest season of my life:
free, my chin as yet unshaved, my
heart still winged with poetry —

deh, l'induca a venire a me per poco:
or son qui solo; e, nella fredda, oscura
notte, la solitudine paura
quasi mi fa. Seduto accanto al foco,
nella prigion di queste quattro mura,

io gli altri me chiamo a convegno. Solo,
fors'egli solo non verrà, che troppo
son io diverso ora da lui: vo zoppo
pe 'l cammin che intraprese egli di volo,
e la trama ch' ei finse or io rattoppo.

II

Silenzio. Gli altri, con le amiche a braccio,
entrano. Come io resterei, se vecchio
mi vedessi d'un tratto in uno specchio,
essi, cosí, dinanzi a me. L'impaccio
vincon prima le donne, e in un orecchio

vien la bruna di Como a dirmi in fretta:
«Tu sai che cosa io sono, ora; ma a lui
non dirne nulla: ei mi vede qual fui!»
Ti basta un sol mio sguardo, o poveretta,
e in un brivido tutta ti rabbuj.

Egli ha guardato me; qual sei ti vede.
Non nasconderti il viso, ché di te
non ha ragione di lagnarsi: in me
vani egli or vede l'amor tuo, la fede
che gli giurava, e vana ombra pur sé.

E tu, Jenny? Ti sei nascosta dietro
la tenda? Piangi? Il magro tuo dottore
mi guarda, come oppresso di stupore.
Da quella neve, da quell'aer tetro
venía la sua magrezza, il suo squallore.

Eh, tu, dottor, lassú donde t'ho tratto,
ree promesse ripeti alla gentile

for pity's sake, urge him to visit me
awhile. Now I am here alone, and in the cold,
dark night the solitude makes me almost
afraid. Sitting by my fire
in the prison of these four walls,

I summon the others to gather. Only he,
perhaps, only he won't come, so
different am I now from him. I limp
down the path he flew along,
and the plot he imagined is patchwork now.

2

Silence. The others, sweethearts on their arms,
enter. They look at me as I'd have looked
if I had seen myself in the mirror suddenly old.
The awkward pause is overcome
by women first. And the dark girl

from Como is quick to whisper in my ear:
"You know what I am now, but say
nothing to him. He sees me as I was!"
One look from me suffices, ah, poor thing,
and with a shudder, darkness swallows you.

He looked at me. He sees what you are.
Don't hide your face. He has no reason
to complain of you. He sees in me
your love is empty and the faith
you pledged him and himself an empty shade.

And you, Jenny? Do you hide behind
the curtain? Crying? Your scrawny scholar
stares at me as if weighed down by wonder.
Out of that snow, that dismal air,
his feebleness has come, his misery.

Eh, you, scholar, up there where I took you,
you repeat false promises to the gentle

compagna. E vedi? Or ella piange. Vile
forse son io? Non tu, piuttosto, matto?
Le ho mandato da Roma un bel monile...

Mi chiedi conto de' tuoi studii? E voi
dei vostri sogni mi chiedete conto?
Vedete, io non mi lagno, non m'adonto
dei lievi o gravi error vostri, che poi
m'han cagionato i danni ch'ora sconto.

Io vedo in voi ciò che ho man man perduto.
Delle perdite sue non s'era intanto
accorto alcun di voi, poi ch'ancor tanto
restava a me da perdere. Or che muto
e vuoto son rimasto, odio il rimpianto.

I capelli? Debbo anche dei capelli
rispondervi? Oh che bei ciuffi avevate
voi tutti: biondi, come il sol d'estate...
Con gli anni, via, via coi sogni anche quelli!
O lasciatemi in pace, andate, andate.

lover. And see? Now she cries. Am I
the coward? Madman, isn't it you?
I sent her a lovely string of beads from Rome....

You call me to account for your studies?
And you all hold me liable for your dreams?
Look here, I don't complain or take offense
at your mistakes, slight or serious, that
caused the injuries I pay for now.

I see in you what I have slowly lost.
Meanwhile, none of you gave thought to his
own losses, since so much still remained
for me to lose. Now that I'm left
silent and empty, I despise regret.

My hair? Must I even answer to you for
my hair? Oh what splendid locks you had,
all of you, blond as summer sun.... Gone with
the years, they too, gone with the dreams!
Oh leave me in peace! Go! Go away!

Leggendo la storia

Sú, allegra, allegra, cara mia! Mi pare
che tu la prenda un po' troppo sul serio.
Delitti, infamie, sí, senza criterio,
impudicizie da strasecolare;

ma gajo papa era Alessandro Borgia,
tranquillo e ingenuo nelle sue nequizie;
tranne quel della donna, senza vizi, e
sobrio, anzi frugale in mezzo all'orgia.

Ebbe per l'oro, è vero, anima lurca,
ma lo spendeva poi, tutto, tal quale.
Né per un papa infin la vedo male
che andasse a caccia vestito alla turca.

Di piú d'un figlio con Vannozza reo,
diede a Vannozza sua piú d'un marito;
ma l'ultimo, il Canal, bravo erudito:
il Polizian gli dedicò l'Orfeo.

Quanti vitelli con moderna clava
accoppa l'uomo e se li mangia? Orbene,
papa Alessandro, accoppator dabbene,
i suoi nemici, non se li mangiava.

Dunque, non mi seccar! Parole amare,
serio comento a questa fantocciata
della vita? Va' là. Carta sprecata.
Ridi meglio, narrando, e lascia fare.

Reading History

Come on, cheer up, my dear. I think
you take this all too seriously.
Crimes, vile deeds, yes, senseless,
shameless acts beyond belief,

but Alessandro Borgia was an amiable pope,
serene and simple in his wickedness,
without a vice except regarding women, modest
too, and even frugal in the midst of orgy.

His soul, it's true, was greedy after gold,
but then he spent it, all of it.
Nor do I think it sinful for a pope
to go out hunting dressed up like a Turk.

Guilty of more than one child with Vannozza,
be gave his Vannozza more than one husband:
the last of them, Canal, a fine scholar.
Poliziano dedicated the *Orfeo* to him.

How many calves does a man slaughter
with a modern club, then eat? Well,
Pope Alessandro, honest slaughterer
of his enemies, did not eat them up.

So then, don't pester me! Bitter words,
sober commentary on this puppet show
of life? Go on. A waste of paper.
Better tell it laughing, and let it go.

Tormenti

Quando in croce Gesú l'anima rese,
   tutta, per un momento,
su la terra in vita si sospese,
sospese anche l'inferno ogni tormento.

Sisifo che per l'erta maledetta
   avea sospinto il masso
fin su l'aspra del colle aguzza vetta,
donde tuttor riprecipita al basso,

fermo, lassú, starsi d'un tratto il vede:
   stupefatto, in un oh!,
fermo, di sasso, anch'egli resta, e fede
al prodigio prestar non sa, non può.

Si guarda attorno, una e due volte scuote
   il macigno che sta;
vi siede e, con le pugna su le gote,
poi domanda a se stesso: — «E or che si fa?» —

Ma sotto, ecco, gli ruzzola il fatale
   sasso di nuovo, ratto
balza egli in pie', lo segue, e: — «Manco male! —
dice. — Almeno cosí, via, m'arrabatto.» —

E, mentre sú per l'erta novamente
   contro il masso si slancia,
tra le doglie, piú là, Tantalo sente
gridare, urlare: — «Ahi Dio! Ahi Dio! la pancia!» —

Aggirandosi come una bufera,
   satollo, il poveretto,
in quella tregua momentanea s'era
di tutto quanto il suo crudel banchetto.

Ed or gemeva: — «Non lo farò piú!
   Beato chi desia
e nulla ottiene mai! Grazia, Gesú!
Sia benedetta la condanna mia!» —

PUNISHMENTS

When Jesus on the cross gave up the ghost,
   all life on Earth
hung, for a moment, in abeyance.
Hell, too, broke off its torments.

Sysiphus, who had pushed the boulder up
   the cursed slope to
the steep and rugged summit of the hill
from where it always rolls back down,

sees it suddenly motionless up there,
   astonished to an oh!
He too is held stock still and doesn't
believe this miracle, he cannot.

He looks around and pushes once or twice
   at the immobile stone.
Then sits on it, and cheeks on fists, he
asks himself: "Now, what shall I do?"

But wait, from under him the fatal stone
   begins to roll again. Instantly he jumps
to his feet after it, and, "It's just as well!"
he says. "Like this, at least, I've something to strive for."

And while, on the slope, he hurls himself
   once more against the stone,
he hears, amid his labors, Tantalus below
shouting, screaming, "Oh God! oh God, my gut!"

Dancing round like a whirlwind,
   the poor devil had crammed himself,
in that momentary lull,
with every scrap of his horrendous feast.

And now he groaned, "Never again!
   How lucky he is who craves
but never gets! Jesus, thanks!
A blessing is my punishment to me!"

Comiato

O vecchia Terra, è vero, e me ne pento;
 riconosco che il torto è tutto mio.
Se da tant'anni il cor piú non me sento
 se non come un fastidio, anzi un rodìo
continuo in petto, e piú non amo, e sono
quasi un tizzone spento, in abbandono,

come puoi tu sembrarmi bella? — "Pensa,
 (potresti dirmi) quando, innamorato
d'una donnetta pallida melensa,
 che ti pareva un angelo calato
dal ciel, dicevi ch'ero tutta un gajo
riso... Eppure, ricordi? era gennajo..."

Sí, sí, ricordo. Tu, povera Terra,
 eri, qual veramente sei, di mali
piena, dilaniata dalla guerra
 perpetua de' tuoi triste animali,
e vecchia e stanca di volgere in tondo
nella stupida macchina del mondo.

Eppure bella — è vero — me sembravi,
 e gli uomini, per quanto esperti e istrutti
d'ogni saggia perfidia, onesti e bravi
 pareanmi — è vero — che prodigio! tutti.
Sí, sí, ricordo, vecchia Terra: vieta,
se puoi, vieta che canti ogni poeta,

se prima innamorato non si sia,
 tal che gli orrori tuoi non veda, sotto
la ridente d'amor dolce malia.
 Io che mi sono senza cuor ridotto,
d'ora innanzi, ti giuro, starò muto;
questo, ti giuro, è l'ultimo saluto.

Envoi

O ancient Earth, it's true, and I regret it:
   I confess the wrong is all in me.
If for many years I've felt in my heart,
   if not a pain, then an endless
gnawing in my breast, and I love no more and am all
but a cold ember, now abandoned,

how can you seem beautiful to me? "Consider
   (you might say), when you loved
a vapid, boring woman
   who seemed to you an angel fallen
out of heaven, you said that I was pure joyful
laughter.… And yet, remember? It was January.…"

Of course, I remember. You, pitiful Earth,
   were what you truly are, full of evils,
agonized by the perpetual war
   among your hopeless creatures,
and old and weary with turning round and round
in the stupid mechanism of the world.

And yet, it's true, you seemed lovely to me,
   and men, however expert and skilled
in every cunning treachery, appeared to me
   honest and decent — what wonders! All of them.
Yes, yes, I remember, ancient Earth: stop
if you can, stop every poet from singing

if he's not in love beforehand,
   so he doesn't see your horrors under
the sweet enchantment of a smiling love.
   I who have shrunk my heart to nothingness,
I swear to you, from this day forward I will be mute,
and this, I swear to you, is a last goodbye.

Poesie Varie

Various Poems (Uncollected)

Il globo

Ecco il globo: una palla di cartone,
che gira attorno a un asse interno. Gira...
Tracciato di color varii, si mira
il confin proprio d'ogni nazione.

Questo, l'Oceano Atlantico; ed è mare
quanto azzurro si vede. Questa soma
di grinze qui, montagne: le Alpi. Roma
è questo punto che pare e non pare.

Chi lo direbbe a prima giunta? Eppure
vi son uomini grandi, anzi immortali,
in questo baloccuccio; grandi mali
e grandi beni e grandi affetti e cure...

Io però me lo tengo tra le mani,
e lo faccio girare con un dito.
Stupido giuoco! Lo facciam finito?
Preparo il finimondo per dimani.

The Globe

Here is the globe: a cardboard ball
that turns around an inner axis. It turns....
Drawn in various colors, every nation's
true boundaries can be seen.

This, the Atlantic Ocean; a sea
as blue as it appears. This clutch
of wrinkles here are mountains: the Alps.
Rome is this point you see and cannot see.

Who could tell at first sight? Yet
great men live there, in fact, immortals,
on this little plaything; great evils
and great goods, great loves, great cares....

I, however, hold it in my hands
and make it turn with one finger.
A stupid game! Should we cut it short?
I'll prepare the world's end for tomorrow.

LIETA

Che m'avviene?
Io piú libero stamane
il respir traggo: perché?
ed al piè
non mi sento piú catene.
Che m'avviene?
Senti? Suonan le campane...
Forse è tutta imbandierata
la città...

Dalla chiusa austerità
delle antiche esauste vene
oggi forse innamorata
sorge Roma a nuova età.
Sia gajezza in tutti i cuori:
calde, franche, gioviali
per le vie suonin parole:
si spalanchin tutte al sole
le finestre ed abbian fiori
su i lucenti davanzali.

Si, lo so: va tutto a rotoli;
senza fede né dottrina,
sotto un vacuo od irto nome,
i pensier nostri slegati
s'avviluppano coi fati
che stan come
nembi sopra una rovina.
Dove io vada?
Non lo so.

Vado dove la mia sorte
mi conduce.
Senza luce
corro anch'io verso la morte.
Ci sarà per la mia strada

Feeling Good

What's happening to me?
I breathe more freely
this morning: why?
And I don't feel chains
on my feet any more.
What's happening to me?
Listen! Bells are ringing....
Maybe the city is all
decked in flags.

Out of the pinched austerity
of its ancient, worn-out veins,
perhaps today Rome is in love
and a new age is dawning.
Let there be joy in every heart.
Let warm, frank, jovial
words resound in the streets,
and the windows be open wide
to the sun, and let them have
flowers on all the shining sills.

Yes, I know, everything's going downhill,
without faith or creed.
Under an empty or crude name
our unconstrained thoughts
are bound up with fates
that wait like
clouds above a ruin.
Where am I going?
I don't know.

I go wherever my destiny
leads me.
In the darkness
I, too, hasten toward death.
There will be a pit on my way

*una fossa in cui cadrò.
Sí, lo so — ma di pensare
non ho tempo, oggi, né voglia:
un inganno ancor germoglia
nel mio cuore, e voglio amare,
voglio ridere, scherzare.
In continui, vaghi errori,
finché sotto il càuto piede
non mi cede
la malferma terra, vo'
di quest'aura inebriarmi,
consolarmi
d'esser nato a questa vita.
Primavera sia fiorita
quando alfin giú me n'andrò,
perch'io possa,
nel cader, baciare i fiori
che celavanmi la fossa.*

into which I will tumble.
Yes, I know that, but I have
no time, right now, to think
about it, nor the wish.
Once again an illusion sprouts
in my heart, and I want to love,
to laugh, to play,
until the shaky ground
gives way
beneath my wary foot.
I want to be drunk on this air,
to console myself
for being been born to this life.
Let spring be in full bloom
when I go down at last,
so that I may, as I fall,
kiss the flowers
that concealed the pit from me.

Amor sincero

I

Lunga speranza e desiderii brevi...
la catena, perché? Troppo gravate
portiam le membra di catene: lievi
ci sieno almen le poche gioje.

Fate,
donne giovani e belle e innamorate,
solo a modo d'un uom che tutte v'ama:
in questa vita breve lunga brama
non nudrite giammai, né vi legate.

Noi sempre andiamo perseguendo un bene,
che dai nostri desiri in fuga è volto;
ma trista veramente chi l'ottiene!

Cogliendo fiori di molti sentieri
corriam la vita! E voi datemi ascolto,
che questi son consigli sani e veri.

II

Io vorrei che le donne graziose
fossero come i fiori d'un giardino.
Io me n'andrei tra le animate rose,
cantando pei viali ogni mattino;

tra lor m'adagerei pianin pianino,
me le vedrei d'attorno, in su lo stelo
chine vêr me, parlarmi davvicino,
e sarei pago del lor dolce anelo.

Poi tutte, ad una ad una, io le côrrei;
mi starebbe ciascuna un dí sul seno,
a godersi i miei baci e i sospir miei.

Oppur nessuna ne vorrei toccare;
vorrei, senza succhiar miele o veleno,
il profumo aspirarne, ed oltre andare.

Sincere Love

1

   Long hope and brief desires....
Why the chains? Our legs carry
too great a burden of chains. At least
our few joys are light. Do,

   young, beautiful, women in love,
do just as a man would who loves you all:
in this brief life never nourish
long desire, nor tie yourselves down.

   We're always running after a prize
that's turned and fled from our desires,
but the one who catches it is truly sad!

   Gathering flowers from many paths,
we race through life! Now listen to me,
these are sound counsels and true.

2

   I would like it if pretty women
were like the flowers in a garden.
I'd stroll among the living roses
singing on the paths each morning.

   I'd lie down among them gently
and see them all around me, leaning
toward me on their stems, confiding in me,
and I would bask in their sweet breath.

   Then one by one I'd pluck them all,
place each one on my breast for a day
to enjoy my kisses and my sighs.

   Or else I would not touch them.
I'd like, without sipping honey or poison,
to breathe their perfume, and then be gone.

Notte insonne

I

Io mi sento guardato da le stelle
e questa notte non posso dormire.
Mi par che qualche cosa esse, sorelle
maggiori, a questa terra voglian dire.

O sorgive di luci, la parola,
la parola tremenda del mistero
ditela a una vegliante anima sola
perduta in mezzo al vostro cielo nero.

II

So che dovrei di ciò ch'è in terra solo
occupar la mia mente e i desir miei;
ma tu piú forte d'ogni intento sei,
ciel che l'anima mia rapisci a volo.

Tutte le fonti della vita insieme
non avran mai poter di saziare
l'ardentissima sete, e sempre amare
avrò le labbra e vigile la speme,

ben che ognora delusa. O di basalto
funebre cielo, invano ti martella
il mio pensiero; invano si ribella
in terra, invano si rifugia in alto.

È l'antica paura, è l'appassito
istinto della fede, o questa nuova
smania, alla quale nessun tetto giova,
che mi spinge a cercar nell'infinito?

Io di qua giú, di questa terra breve,
di cui ben sento la viltà dinnanti

Sleepless Nights

1

   I feel watched by the stars,
and I cannot sleep tonight.
They seem, elder sisters,
to want to speak to this earth.

   O springs of light, the word,
the tremendous word of the mystery,
say it to a wakeful soul alone,
lost in the depths of your black sky.

2

   I know that I should occupy my mind
and my desires only with earthly things,
but you are mightier than all desire,
heaven, that suddenly ravishes my soul.

   All the springs of life
together will never satisfy
this burning thirst. My lips forever will
be bitter, and vigilant my hope,

   though always disappointed. O funereal
and basalt sky, vainly my mind
assaults you. Vainly it rebels
on earth. Vainly it seeks refuge on the heights.

   Is it the ancient fear, is it the faded
instinct of faith, or this new
craving, for which no shelter avails,
that goads me on to search the infinite?

   I am of here below, of this brief earth,
and know full well its lowliness before

a te, che cerco? — Un suon di chiari canti
dal bujo vien della vicina pieve.

Si prega lí, si prega per la vita
e per la morte; ardon votivi ceri
su un altar ben parato e gl'incensieri
fuman sotto un'imagine scolpita.

A chi mentí la vita, a chi la terra
non concesse una sola primavera,
a chi riposo non cercò la sera,
ma il tempo, senza tregua, o insidie o guerra,

tu solamente, o ignoto ciel, rimani;
e a te su i sassi della terra infida
ogni dolore s'inginocchia e grida:
lacriman gli occhi e tremano le mani.

III

Alla porta del sogno in cui, riparo
a gli amor miei cercando, mi son chiuso,
siccome in un castello aurato e chiaro
qual le fate inalzarne aveano in uso,

batton le cure pallide, impedite
le membra da un intrico di catene;
«Il mondo ti reclama: apri. L'immite
ora ti vieta un solitario bene»;

batton, pregando esaudimento, i brevi
desiderî, e tentandomi: «È qua giú
la tua radice: se per lei non bevi,
cadrà la cima ove t'annidi tu»;

e batton i bisogni, delle cure
ancor piú schiavi: «Apri: sfuggir non puoi
al comun fato. Giú, folle, tu pure,
la tua catena a trascinar fra noi.»

you. What am I searching for? — A sound of pure song
comes in the darkness from the parish church nearby.

   They pray in there, they pray for life,
for death. They kindle votive candles
on a sumptuous altar and the censers
smoke below a sculptured image.

   To one deceived by life, to whom the earth
has granted not a single Spring,
who does not look for rest at evening,
but time without truce, either as sham or as war,

   only you remain, O unknown sky,
and every grief kneels to you
on the stones of the faithless earth, and cries:
the eyes shed tears and the hands tremble.

3

   At the gate of dreams where,
seeking refuge in my loves, I've shut myself,
as in a gilt and gleaming castle
like those the fairies used to raise,

   pale Troubles knock, their legs
bound in a tangle of chains:
"The world demands you: open up. The pitiless
hour forbids a solitary good."

   Transient Desires knock, begging
satisfaction and tempting me: "Down here
is your root. If you don't drink by it,
the heavens will fall on your hiding place."

   And Needs, still more the slaves of Care,
knock: "Open up. You cannot flee
the common fate. Come down, fool, you too
must drag your chain among us."

V

*L'anima or segue nella notte il fiume
che dal grembo di Roma già silente,
siccome enorme placido serpente,
svolgesi della Luna al freddo lume.*

*Chiama da lungi con assidua voce
il tenebroso palpitante mare;
l'anima pensa al vano suo passare,
s'affretta il fiume alla solvente foce.*

5

   Like a vast and placid serpent
the river flows at night from the lap
of silent Rome, and as it unwinds in the moon's
cold light, the soul follows after it.

   From afar, the shadowy, heaving sea
calls with an unceasing voice:
the soul broods on its vain passage,
the river rushes to its dissolution.

LA VIA

> *Provar per ogni via*
> *come la nostra vita a caso sia.*

I

Mi trovo qui per caso, di passaggio.
Vi starò quanto men vi potrò stare.
Non che m'annoj, tutt'altro! Anzi il viaggio
m'ha divertito. Ma è pur forza andare.

Dormia, venendo, io dico, e che perciò
che modo per venire e che via tenni
e donde sia venuto ora non so.
Ma poco importa: da una parte venni.

Dove andrò? Non lo so... Ahi, neppur questo!
Ma poco importa: andrò dove che sia.
Quel che piú val è che si faccia presto:
guardarsi attorno, e scegliersi una via.

II

Facile a dire, sceglersi una via!
   Di vie, ce ne son tante qui. Però
      quale sarà la mia?
E come farmi un qualche itinerario,
   se finora non so
perché venni, onde venni, dove andrò?
Son cose che si sanno d'ordinario,
quando per un viaggio ci s'avvia.

IV

Concepito ho il grave dubbio,
   ch'io sia solo a non capire

The Way

> To test in every way
> what our life may chance to be.

1

I'm here by chance, passing through.
  I'll stay as briefly as I can.
  Not that I'm bored, just the reverse! The journey
  has in fact amused me. But one must go on.

Getting here, I confess, I slept, so
  how I came, and the way I took,
  and where I'm from, I don't now know.
  It doesn't matter. I came from somewhere.

Where headed? I don't know.... Alas, not even that!
  But no matter. I'll go somewhere.
  What is important is to act quickly:
  look around and choose oneself a path.

2

Easy to say, choose oneself a path!
  There are many paths here. But
      which one will be mine?
And how to make some sort of itinerary,
  since up to now I don't know
why I've come, from where, and where I'm headed?
These things are usually known
when one sets out on a journey.

4

I have conceived the solemn doubt
  that I am the only one among mankind

la mia sorte in mezzo agli uomini...
Certa gente fa stupire!

Non può credersi, guardandola,
che non sia convinta a pieno,
che bisogna restar bestie
per tirare in pace, almeno...

Io mi perdo in vuote indagini
e dimentico la via...
Che la stoffa in me, Dio liberi,
d'un filosofo ci sia?

VI

Smarrito, smarrito... A guardare
mi sto la gente che viene e che va.
Trascinami l'onda, e a virare
di qua mi passa, perplesso, e di là.

Ma par che ognuno sicuro se 'n vada
ad una meta sicura laggiù...
Vi sono forse lí in fondo a la strada?
E ci si va per non sorger mai piú?

VII

Ora ho chiesto a piú d'un savio
pe 'l mio mal qualche consiglio.
M'intronarono di chiacchiere
molti, ed un mi disse: «Figlio,

che ho da dirti? È bene fingerci
qualche cosa innanzi a noi
che ci faccia andar, fantasima
o fantoccio, è uguale! E poi...

poi raggiungerlo. È ne l'ansia
del raggiungere la vita.
Ché il fantoccio cangia immagine
spesso, appena è tra le dita.»

who does not understand his destiny....
Certain people make one wonder!

It's impossible not to believe, seeing them,
　that they're absolutely sure
　we must keep on being beasts,
　plodding along as quietly as we can....

I lose myself in empty speculation
　and cannot remember the way....
　Can it be that, God forbid,
I have the makings of a philosopher?

6

Lost, lost...I stand
　and watch the people come and go.
　The wave drags me and wrenches me around,
　bewildered, this way and that.

It seems each one is sure of himself and
　is going to a certain goal out there....
　Are these, perhaps, at the road's end?
　And does one go there never to return?

7

I've asked of more than one wise man
　advice about what ails me.
　They deafened me with endless babble,
　and one said to me, "My son,

what can I tell you? It's best to pretend
　there's something before us
　that makes us go on, figment
　or puppet, it's all the same! And then...

then pursue it. Life is in
　the uncertainty of pursuit,
　for the puppet often changes shape
　as soon as you catch hold of it."

Alba

Vedi tu come, non ancor dal fumo
dei pensieri il cervello annebbiato,
al tuo spirito (l'alba t'ha destato)
io vita, io mondo un altro aspetto assumo?

Ti parlerò meglio all'aperto: vieni!
fuori le porte de l'a te funesta
città! Slarga il tuo petto intanto a questa
aura ristoratrice. Ecco i miei beni:

l'aria, il verde, la luce... non le case
degli uomini ammucchiate! non le oscure
chiese, o le sedi socïali impure,
d'ogni viltà, d'ogni miseria invase!

Ben venga a te, che questa mane, avanti
che il sol nascesse, abbandonavi il letto;
e fuori or vieni insolito diletto
a trâr da me, come da strani incanti.

Guarda! Nel sogno de la terra assorti,
sorgono a l'aria gli alberi: li scuote
invano il vento, invano li percuote
la pioggia... Forte, come lor son forti,

non sei tu in me! Nel grembo mio profondo
stendi le tue radici. Tu potrai
vivermi sempre, non morir giammai,
abbracciar tutto e divenire il mondo!

Non tendi a questo? Gli alberi tue membra
saran; la terra, il corpo; in ogni fiume
le tue vene, il tuo spirito nel lume
del dí vedrai... Già divenir ti sembra

quel che vedi... Lo senti? Orbene, questo
che tu senti son io: sono te stesso;

Dawn

Dawn has waked you. Now that the fog
of thoughts no longer clouds your brain,
do you see how I life, I world,
assume another aspect to your spirit?

I will make better sense to you in the open: come!
Come outside the gates of the city, so fatal
to you! Fill your chest with this invigorating
air. Here are my precious things:

the air, the verdure, the light.... Not men's
houses all heaped up, nor the darkened
churches, nor the squalid offices,
corrupted by every cowardice and filth!

Give thanks that in this early morning, before
the rising of the sun, you left your bed,
as if under a strange spell, to come
outside and take a rare delight from me.

Look! In the dream of the sleeping earth
trees rise into the air, the wind
vainly shakes them, vainly the rain beats
down on them.... You are not as strong in me

as they are strong! Spread your roots
in my deep womb. You can live in me
forever, you will never die.
Embrace it all and so become the world!

Isn't this what you desire? The trees will be
your arms and legs, the earth your body, in every
river your veins. You will see your spirit
in the light of day.... Already you're becoming

what you see. Do you feel it? Good. What
you feel is me. I am you yourself.

*di me tu vivi, io di te vivo. Adesso
ritorna in mezzo agli uomini modesto,*

*ne la città rientra. Primavera
nuova presto verrà. Bisbiglia intanto
a chi ti passa triste e fosco a canto,
come un augurio, ne l'orecchio: — Spera.*

You live in me. I live in you. Now
humbly go back among mankind,

return to the city. A new spring
soon will come. Meanwhile, whisper
to whomever passes you by, sad and sullen,
like a good augury in his ear: Have hope.

Esame (1895)

Concreta, esprimi il tuo desio: che vuoi?
— *Nulla!* — *E la pace tuttavia ti manca...*
Perché pace non hai? — *L'anima è stanca!* —
Stanca di che? di che soffrir tu puoi?

Non della vita: tu non vivi — *guardi*
la vita, e indaghi: ecco il tuo mal! Bisogna
non indagar; ma oprar, vivere. Sogna
altri rimedî la tua mente? È tardi,

è tardi, e invano! Tu non guarirai.
Ama, lavora, se già cener tutto
il tuo cuore non è. Giú, giú nel flutto...
Perché a guardarlo dalla sponda stai?

Torbido è il flutto, è vero; e molti, oh molti
in esso si dibattono, e già stanno
per finir senz'ajuto; ahi, piú non hanno
lena, li vedi? Oh disperati volti!

Salva, se puoi, qualcuno! Ajuta! ajuta!
Cerchi uno scopo? Or questo sia lo scopo!
Cessa dal vano dimandare: — *E dopo?* —
Con lor perisci, e sia l'inchiesta muta...

Examination (1895)

Specifically, what's your desire, what do you want?
"Nothing!" Yet you're not at peace....
Why are you without peace? "My soul is weary!"
Weary of what? What do you suffer from?

Not of life. You don't live, you look
at life and question. There's your trouble! You
must not question, but act, live. Does your mind
dream of other remedies? It's late,

too late and futile! You won't get better.
Love, work, if your heart is not yet
turned to ashes. Go down, down into the flow....
Why do you stay on the shore looking on?

The flow is murky, true, and many, oh many
flounder in it, and already helpless have
almost given up. Alas, most have no
strength. See them? Oh the despairing faces!

Save someone if you can! Help! Help!
Do you seek a purpose? Then this be the purpose!
Give up vain questioning. "And then?"
Perish with them, and let the questioning be stilled....

Approdo

E al fine, eccomi in porto. Ancor mi resta
negli occhi uno stupor truce, una truce
visione, il terror de la tempesta;
ma svaniran ne la tranquilla luce.

È certo, intanto, che son salvo, in porto.
Logorato, ma salvo. Arida sponda
e inamabile è questa; è vero: morto
però a lei mi potea trascinar l'onda.

Tutto il tesor che meco avea l'ha il mare.
E pur travolta giacque la persona
più cara a me, né la potei salvare:
ombra mi seguirà che non perdona.

Ma vinsi la tempesta e in porto or sono;
so la fortuna del viaggio fosco:
signor di me, non fo di me più dono,
e la mia fredda volontà conosco.

Landing

And at last, here I am in port. My eyes
are still dazed with wonder, a fearsome
vision, the terror of the storm,
but it fades in the peaceful light.

For now, it's certain that I am safe in port.
Worn out, but safe. An empty,
inhospitable beach — it's true — but the waves
might have dragged me here dead.

The sea now has all that I owned.
And then the person dearest to me
swept away. I could not save her.
A shadow pursues me that does not forgive.

But I have conquered the storm and am now in port.
I know the risks of the dark voyage.
Master of myself, I will give myself to no one,
and I know my own cold will.

Torna, Gesù!

La memoranda notte è ormai vicina
e mi risuona ancora negli orecchi,
eco gentil dell'età mia bambina,
la voce de' miei vecchi:
« Candido, roseo e biondo
come, nato da giorni, eri anche tu,
vien questa notte al mondo
il Bambino Gesú!»

Ogn'anno, ogn'anno, in questo freddo mese,
per quanto stanca, l'anima risogna
la festa che a Gesú fa il mio paese.
Già suona la zampogna...
Ah, che profonda, arcana
malinconia, che nostalgia m'assal
della casa lontana,
del villaggio natal!

Rigide sere della pia novena
in cui, sur ogni piazza, in ogni via,
fiamman, fuochi gregal, fasci d'avena;
mentre la litania
il vicinato intuona
raccolto innanzi a un rustico altarin,
e la zampogna suona,
tintinna l'acciarin.

Ed io, fanciullo, a la finestra dietro
me ne stavo, e schiarendo con un dito
timidamente l'appannato vetro,
rimiravo smarrito,
in un'ansia segreta,
se in quella notte piena di mister
la fulgida cometa
apparisse davver...

Jesus, Come Back!

   The memorable night is now at hand
and there again sounds in my ears
the soft echo of my childhood,
the voice of my elders:
"White, pink, and blond
like you, born not long ago,
into the world there comes this night
the Infant Jesus!"

   Every year, every year, in this cold month,
however weary, my soul dreams again
the holiday for Jesus in my village.
Already the bagpipe sounds....
Ah, what profound, mysterious
sorrow, what homesickness
for that distant house,
that village where I was born!

   Frigid evenings of the pious novena
when, in every square and every street,
there were fires burning, and sheaves of oats,
while the neighbors,
gathered before a rustic
altar, intoned the litany,
and the bagpipe sounded,
the flint stones clinked.

   And I, a small boy, stood at
a window, and wiping with a finger
the misted-over glass,
looked out confusedly,
in secret anxiety
whether on that night of mystery
the brilliant comet
would really appear....

E dubitavo allora, e ho dubitato
sempre, dappoi. S'inaridí l'istinto
della fede nel cuore: errai bendato
per questo labirinto
della vita mortale,
e te pure chiamai causa, Gesú,
d'una parte del male
che si soffre quaggiú.

Ma santa adesso appar la tua follia
anche al mio sguardo, o dolce redentore.
E torna, io prego, a noi, torna, Messia,
a predicar l'amor;
torna con la man pura
a battere alle porte infime ancor,
dove una gente oscura
di fame e freddo muor!

Altri, del rosso tuo mantello avvolto,
d'odio nudrendo la gentil parola,
batte alle oscure case, e infosca il volto
de la miseria. Vola
il grido della guerra...
Pace tu sei, Gesú, tu sei pietà;
torna a rifare in terra
d'amor la carità.

And I doubted then, and have doubted
ever since. The instinct of faith
dried up in my heart: I wandered blindfolded
through this labyrinth of mortal life,
and even blamed you, Jesus,
for some part of the evil
that is suffered here below.

   But now your folly appears divine
even to my eyes, O sweet Redeemer.
Come back, I beg you, come back to us, Messiah,
to preach love.
Come back with your pure hand
to knock again at the humblest doors
where obscure folk
die of hunger and cold.

   Others, wrapped in your red mantle,
fostering hate with your kind word,
knock at lowly houses and darken
the face of poverty. Already
the cry of war takes flight....
You are peace, Jesus, you are pity.
Come back to earth and again make
charity from love.

Esame (1896)

Forse perché lo guardo da una faccia
che piange; n'ha poi tante, e non è brutto
né bello, per se stesso: è il mondo, e tutto
dipende da qual parte ognun si faccia

a contemplarlo. È ver che a me giammai
non rise; ma vi son pur tanti, ai quali
ride spesso e nasconde i propri mali.
Io con l'occhio malevolo il guardai

sempre, da che son nato. Or ne la vista
delle cose vorrei dimenticare
me stesso, il pensier mio; vorrei lavare
d'ogni memoria in lei l'anima trista.

Del proprio sogno uscir non è concesso.
Chi l'ombre al sogno appresta? Ognuno sotto
un vario inganno aggirasi: io vi lotto
contro i fantasmi miei, contro me stesso.

Examination (1896)

Maybe because I look at its tearful
aspect — it has many others and is neither ugly
nor beautiful in itself — it is the world, and
everything depends on the angle from which

one contemplates it. It's true that for me it never
smiled, but for many others it often
laughs and hides its innate evils.
Ever since I was born I've regarded it

with a distrustful eye. Now I have seen
things in it that I would like to forget myself,
my own thoughts. I would cleanse
the spirit of sadness from every memory.

One may not escape from one's dream.
Who gives the dream its darkness? Everyone
makes his way under a different illusion. I struggle
against my phantoms, against myself.

L'ABBANDONO

Tu che intender mi puoi, leggi e perdona.

I

Intenderà, pensavo: oggi o dimani
intenderà: dietro il mio breve addio
la porta chiuderà con le sue mani.

Non staran certo eternamente assorte
l'anime nostre nel primo desio,
mute a vegliar di questo amor la morte.

Forse la spingerà l'ombra che lenta
avanza, sotto i nostri occhi, sul suolo,
o la fontana che giú si lamenta,

o qualche mio sospir non ben represso,
o il batter tetro del mio vecchio oriuolo,
la memoria d'un favor concesso.

La porta chiuderà con le sue mani.

II

E le parlai cosi, piú d'una volta:

Meglio che tu mi lasci al mio destino.
Misera meco non ti voglio. Ascolta.
Solo io prosegua il mio triste cammino.

Innanzi agli occhi miei pose la sorte
una meta lontana e tutta avvolta
di nebbie sí, che insidia par di morte.

Tra i dubbî or tu del mio sentier malfido
certo venir non puoi: tu, cosí fina
e candida, lasciare il tuo bel nido...

Piangi? Ebben, piangi. Io non dirò: Cammina!

An Ending

> You who can understand me, read and forgive.

1

She will understand, I thought, today or tomorrow
she will understand. After my brief goodbye
she will close the door with her hands.

It's clear that our souls will not remain
eternally absorbed in their earlier desire,
mutely observing the death of this love.

Perhaps the shadow that slowly advances
before our eyes on the ground will prod her,
or the fountain that complains below,

or an ill-repressed sigh of mine,
or the dismal ticking of my old watch,
or the memory of a favor granted.

She will close the door with her hands.

2

And I said this to her more than once:

It's best that you leave me to my fate.
I don't want you to be miserable with me. Listen.
I will make my sad way alone.

I see my destiny before me,
a distant goal all clouded
by mists so that it seems a deadly snare.

Amid such doubts you surely cannot follow
my uncertain path, you, so delicate
and pure, to leave your beautiful nest....

You're crying? Well, cry. I will not say, Go away!

III

Pur tu me segui ancora, ombra dolente.
L'oscura soglia dell'oblio varcare
dunque non vuoi con le memorie care,
e sempre e ovunque mi starai presente?

Se di te la memoria affligger tanto
mi deve, ah meglio è forse ch'io ritorni
teco a soffrir l'antica pena e i giorni
stanchi e il tuo chiuso inconsolabil pianto.

E non più questo avido assedio muto
di un'ombra che mi spia, che tutto vede
entro di me pria ch'io lo senta e chiede
di perpetuo compianto al cor tributo.

IV

Se con mano tremante (e già la mano
al pensiero mi trema) alla tua porta
battessi e all'improvviso, aprendo piano,
tu mi vedessi innanzi a te nel vano
della soglia — stupita, incerta, smorta!

Odo del tuo stupore il grido: acuto,
breve. Degli occhi tuoi vedo lo sguardo
e il tremor delle labbra. Qual saluto
ti porgerei? Restar potessi muto!
e tu potessi intendere com'ardo...

Come immemore tu dell'abbandono
parlar dovresti, qual chi indulga. Intento
io rifarei l'amor seguendo il suono
della tua voce. Tacito al perdono
risponderebbe certo il pentimento.

No, non verrò. Nel pallido tuo seno
è pure un cuore come il mio che geme,

3

Yet you haunt me still, sorrowful shade.
You will not cross the dark threshhold
to oblivion with your precious memories.
Will you always and everywhere stay present to me?

If the memory of you must trouble me
so much, ah, maybe it's better that I return
to you to suffer the old pain and wearisome
days and your suppressed, inconsolable tears

and no longer endure this silent, tenacious siege
by a shadow that spies on me, that sees everything
within me before I know of it and demands
the tribute of my heart's perpetual grief.

4

If with a trembling hand — and already
my hand trembles at the thought —
I should unexpectedly knock at your door,
and slowly opening, you would see me
before you and be dumbstruck, uncertain, faint.

I hear your cry of surprise, sharp, quick.
I see the look in your eyes and the quivering
of your lips. What greeting should I give you?
Would that I might remain silent!
And that you might understand how I burn....

How could you speak as if oblivious
to our break-up, like one who forgives? I would
be determined to revive our love at the sound
of your voice. Dumb at being pardoned,
I would surely feel repentance.

No, I will not go. In your bosom,
pale and pure, there is a heart like mine

un cuor che brama di lagnarsi, pieno
di lagrime, d'angoscia, di veleno.
Verrei per tormentarci ancora insieme?

V

Quand'io tornai d'un altro amor già stanco
a lei che m'attendea presaga e sola,
tutto dinnanzi le restai, ma franco
fu quel silenzio, piú d'ogni parola.

v«Finalmente ritorni!» ella mi disse.
«Neppur m'hai dato annunzio del ritorno...»
E su me le pupille intense e fisse
tenea nell'ombra. Già moriva il giorno.

Ah come intanto mi stringea la manno!
D'assedio m'opprimean tutti i suoi sensi
spiandomi. — «Non parli?» — E invano,
invano di parlar mi sforzavo. — «A che mai pensi?»

Ed io pensavo. Ancora non le ho detto
la parola che attende. È come morta
la mia man nella sua, morto nel petto
il mio cuore per lei. Non se n'è accorta?

Mi cinse a un tratto il collo, lievemente.
«Perché non m'ami piú, perché?» — mi chiese.
Ed alitarmi in volto la dolente
voce sentii. Non pianse ella: mi prese

la testa e su le labbra arse la mia
bocca si strinse a lungo, a lungo, forte...
Ah, niun può dir che cosa atroce sia
baciar chi brucia, con le labbra morte!

that groans, a heart that longs to complain,
full of tears, of anguish, of poison.
Should I come to torment us both again?

5

When I, already tired of another love, came back
to her who waited for me, ominous and alone,
I stood before her, but the silence
spoke more frankly than any words.

"Finally, you come back!" she said to me.
"You didn't even tell me in advance.…"
And from the shadows her eyes gazed at me
intense and fixed. The day was already dying.

Ah, how she gripped my hand meanwhile!
All her senses were fastened oppressively
upon me. "You don't speak?" And helplessly
I tried to make myself speak. "What are you thinking?"

And I thought. I still had not uttered
the word she waited for. It's as if dead,
my hand in hers, my heart dead to her
in my breast. Wasn't she aware of it?

Suddenly she put her arm around my neck lightly,
"Why don't you love me anymore, why?" she asked.
And her breath on my face, I heard
her mournful voice. She did not cry. She took

my head and on my dry lips
she pressed for a long time, hard.…
Ah, no one can tell what a terrible thing it is
to kiss burning lips with lips that are dead!

VI

Accendi il lume nella stanza triste;
alle finestre il ciel grigio s'oscura.
O con piacer la tua mestizia assiste
al morire del dí? Non hai paura?

Sei sola. L'ombra già t'avvolge densa.
Chi parla a te da un tempo ormai lontano?
Io t'ho ingannata e abbaandonata... Pensa
forse a questo il tuo cuor? Tu piangi invano.

Nulla io dar ti potea, piú nulla; e un bene
fu per te certo il mio tardo abbandono.
Tenti come uno scampo a ree catene
questo dolor: concedi a me perdono.

Senti quanta tristezza è nel cuor mio?
Vedi in che notte il mio spirito è avvolto?
Libera sei! Ch'hai tu perduto? Oblio
stendi su un sogno che sta ben sepolto.

6

You light the lamp in your sad room.
At the windows the gray sky grows dark.
Or are you content that your sadness helps
the day to die? Aren't you afraid?

You're alone. Dense shadow already envelops you.
Who speaks to you from a time now long past?
I deceived you and abandoned you…is your
heart perhaps thinking of this? You weep in vain.

Nothing, I could give you nothing more, and
for you my desertion was surely a blessing.
Try to escape from the heavy chains
of this suffering: grant me pardon.

Do you know how much sadness is in my heart?
Do you see the night that encloses my spirit?
You are free! What have you lost? Draw
forgetfulness over a dream that is buried for good.

Primo rintocco

Levo ogni tanto dal guancial la testa
a spiar tra le imposte. È bujo ancora.
Ma invan gli occhi richiudo, che, già desta,
  l'anima intorno tutto mi colora
della sua luce tediosa e mesta.
Chi per il pan sei stanchi dí lavora
oggi può ben chiuder gli orecchi a questa
  sveglia del gallo che ha cantato or ora.
Ma per il mio lavor mai non è festa.

Quantunque irto mi sia di smanie il letto,
  non vienmi alcuno dalla vita impulso
a levarmi sí presto, e l'alba aspetto.
  Libri di là m'attendono: compulso
da vane forze, il mio pensier dispetto
  vi smania, sí, ma fuor d'essi piú insulso
spettacol m'offre oggi la vita; in petto
  cresce lo sdegno che da lei m'ha espulso,
né alcuna piú m'attira esca d'affetto.

Don... — nel silenzio batte una campana,
  e il suon nel bujo spandesi, ronzando.
Balzo ora e sento un'angosciosa e strana
  voglia d'accorrer, come ad un comando;
ma non a questo: a una chiesa lontana...
  Ah, la rivedo! mi chiamava, quando
andavo anch'io, fanciullo, a messa: arcana
  voce profonda, che destava, ondando,
quell'oscura viuzza suburbana.

Tremar mi sento in petto quella mia
  fede ingenua d'allora accesa ai ceri
che, nella chiesa buja, una malía
  diffondevano insiem con gl'incensieri
fumanti e i rombi della cantoria...

First Chime

Every now and then I raise my head from the pillow
   to peek through the blinds. It's still dark.
But it's hopeless to close my eyes again. Already
   awake, my spirit colors everything around me
with its dreary and melancholy light.
   Those who exhaust themselves working
for bread can easily close their ears to the
   wake-up call of the cock that crowed just now,
but there's no holiday for my labor.

However beset by the restlessness of bed,
   no impulse of life comes to me
to get me up so early, and I wait for dawn.
   Over there books lie waiting for me.
I make futile efforts to read. My nervous
   mind grows restless, but apart from them
life offers me only a duller spectacle, and
   in my breast the disdain grows that
has excluded me from her. No one draws me
   any longer with the bait of affection.

Dong...a bell chimes in the silence,
   and the sound spreads buzzing in the darkness.
I jump up now and feel a strange and anguished
   wish to hurry as if at a command,
but not the tolling of this bell, rather that of a distant
       church....
   Ah, I see it now! It called me when
I, still a small boy, went to mass, a mysterious
   deep voice that aroused in its waves of sound
that dark suburban lane.

I feel my innocent faith of that time
   tremble in my breast, lighted by candles
that diffused an enchantment in the dark
   church, together with the smoking
incense burners and clatter of the choir stalls....

*O donne avvolte negli scialli neri,
che andate in fretta a la chiesuola pia,
attossicato da negri pensieri
è morto il bimbo che con voi venia.*

  O women wrapped in your black shawls,
who hurry to join the pious company,
   poisoned by black thoughts
the little boy is dead who went with you.

Esame (1906)

I

Che so di me? So quel che il tempo vuole
e quanto gli altri vogliono ch'io sappia.
— «Ti tengo! Ed il mio nodo non si scappia, —
mi grida il tempo: — Tu farai parole.
Sfuggi all'ozio? La noija t'accalappia!»
Oh violente smanie, rabbioso
affanno tra le futili catene,
in cui le forze logoro! Mi viene
spesso dai vecchi il mònito amoroso:
— «Figliuolo, è sempre tempo di far bene!

Soltanto a chi fa ben la vita piace!» —
Sí; ma ben altri al giovenil mio foco
incentivi ben altri, o vecchi, invoco.
Oltraggio sembra l'umiltà, la pace.
a me cui tutto appar misero e poco.

II

Pure, il bene, io lo fo. Nel farlo, sento
che fo bene. Da un tenero tremore
n'ho prova, entro di me. Sollevo un mento,
chiudo una man con l'obolo, ed al cuore
altrui, do, quanto posso, esaudimento.

Del mal che temo d'aver fatto, spesso
mi dolgo e pento. Non di men talvolta
scusarmi tenta o l'amor proprio stesso
o la ragion del caso. Il cuore ascolta
la scusa e poi dimentica, rimesso.

Questo è di tutti. Ma chi in petto viva
e costante del ben tiene e del male
la norma? Chi non cangia estimativa

Examination (1906)

1

What do I know of myself? I know what the times want
and as much as others want me to know.
"I've got you!" so cry the times, "and there's no escape
from my grip! You will make words.
Do you flee idleness? Boredom will trap you!"

Oh violent agitations, furious
straining bound in futile chains
where my strength is drained away. Often
my elders send me a loving warning:
"Young man, it's always time for doing good!

Life is pleasing only to those who do good!"
Yes, but in the fire of my youth, O elders,
I appeal to quite other inducements.
Humility, peace, seem an indignity
to me. Everything appears poor and small.

2

Still, I do good. Doing it, I feel that
I'm doing good. From a slight shiver
that I feel within, I lift my chin,
close a hand with an offering, and give
the hearts of others as much relief as I can.

For the bad that I fear I've done, I often
feel sorry and repentant. Nevertheless,
sometimes my pride or my reason tries
to make excuses for me. My heart hears
the excuse and then forgets, restored.

Everyone is like this. But who keeps alive
and constant in his breast the norm
of good and evil? Who doesn't change his judgment

come volgano i casi? E il ben che vale,
se il cuore a concepir Dio non arriva?

III

Io fui tratto con urti violenti
alla terga, cosí, fuor d'ogni via,
bendato. E tanti insiem con me. Lamenti,
bestemmie udii nel bujo mio, la mia
anima intese altre anime dolenti.

Solo! E gli altri ove sono? Io dove sono?
E che mi giova che mi sia caduta
la benda a un tratto qui? Non luce o suono
qui, ma piú bujo entro la notte muta.
Contro chi l'ira o a chi chieder perdono?

M'apparirai tu qui, tremendo Iddio?
qui la paura mi farà cadere
su i ginocchi, prostrato? e il senno mio
vacillerà? qui tutte le chimere
mi tenteranno dal rimosso oblio?

IV

Navi ho veduto per lontani mari
sul tramonto salpar lente dal porto.
Ho salutato anch'io remoti fari,
passando, e so che sian pena e sconforto
nel lasciare la patria e i propri carî.

Ho udito il vento piangermi tre anni
dell'arsa gola di stranier camino,
la solitudin mia pianger, gli affanni
senza conforti e il vario mio destino,
fabbricator di dolorosi inganni.

as situations change? And what is the good worth
if the heart fails to conceive of God?

3

I was pulled down by violent blows
to my back, far from the straight way,
and blindfolded. And many others with me. Groans,
curses, I heard in my darkness. My
soul was aware of other souls in pain.

Alone! And what's become of the others? Where am I?
And what good is it that the blindfold
has suddenly fallen off here? No light or sound
but even more darkness in the hushed night.
Anger against whom? Beg pardon from whom?

Will you appear to me here, O terrible God?
Will fear make me fall
to my knees prostrate? And my mind
will it fail me? Will all the chimeras here
tempt me with repressed forgetfulness?

4

I have seen ships set out for distant seas
Slowly, leave port at sunset.
I, too, have greeted remote beacons
in passing, and I know how dreary and despondent
it is to leave one's country and dear ones.

I have heard the wind moan for three years
in the dry throat of a foreign chimney,
my tears in solitude, the comfortless
anxieties and the vagaries of my destiny,
fabricator of painful deceptions.

Ho raggiunto desíi lunghi,, e le lotte
mi piacquero per loro, o mi fur dure.
Molte speranze dalla sorte rotte
m'ebbi anzi tempo o spente dalle cure,
ladre del sonno, furie della notte.

Ho provato l'amor docile e puro,
le fantastiche febbri del desio
insodisfatto, l'odio d'un sicuro
tradimento, le smanie e poi l'oblio;
stanco ora e mesto, ora ostinato e duro.

Seppi come spontaneo ai mesti nasce
bisogno di mentir nel petto oppresso.
Mi fu dolce sentir salde le fssce
su la ferita e star molle e dimesso
dopo un malor, sena desíi né ambasce.

E lente le speranze, e ognor seguace
a ogni goduto ben lo sdegno; pure
la sete sempre d'altri beni, e pace
mai; fatto un passo, altri bisogni, e cure
vane per un'idea sempre fallace.

Una greve paura indefinita
ora m'ha vinto ed una smaniosa
noja. Ove andar? qual sogno a sé m'invita?
Già molto errai, già so forse ogni cosa.
Or dunque, e dopo? È tutta qui la vita?

Ov'è la vita? Questa ch'io provai
Tant'anni mossa da varia fortuna?
E cosí triste m'ha lasciato? e ormai
se gli occhi avran qualche stupor, nessuna
meraviglia avrà l'anima piú mai?

I have achieved long-held desires and
liked the struggles for them, hard as they were.
Many hopes were shattered early on
by fortune or extinguished by cares,
the thieves of sleep, furies of the night.

I have known love, gentle and pure,
the fantastic fevers of unsatisfied desire,
the hatred of a certain betrayal, the frenzies
and then the forgetting, now weary
and sad, now stubborn and hard.

I learned how to the downhearted
the need to lie is spontaneously born.
It was sweet to feel the tight bandage
on the wound and be weak and submissive
after fainting without desires or anguish.

And gradually I came to despise the hopeful
and the pursuers of every pleasure,
and the constant thirst for new satisfactions,
and peace never, with every step taken
new needs, vain cares for an always illusory idea.

Now a grievous undefined fear
has overcome me, and a restless boredom.
Where shall I go? What dream calls to me?
Already I have drifted much and perhaps
know everything. So much for now, and later?

Is this all of life? Where is life? Is it this that I
have experienced for so many years with changing
fortune? And that has left me so sad?
And now that my eyes have become somewhat
glazed, will my soul never again witness a miracle?

TENUI LUCI IMPROVVISE

I. Crollo

Rido se vedo un bimbo che la mano
schiuda nel vuoto,
credendo di posarvi un qualche oggetto;
non rido piú se noto
che a me pur similmente
accade che nel vano
del tempo crolli ogni desio nascente,
ogni nascente affetto.

II. Per via

— Lascia... Che importa?
— No: resta! Io voglio!
Sempre cosí, sempre in me questa guerra
tra l'Anima, del ciel figlia, e l'Orgoglio,
insolente monello della terra.

III. Giro tondo

Le pagliuzze, i relitti della via,
esposti alla mercé di chi cammina,
hanno anch'essi nel mondo
il lor breve momento d'allegria:
viene un soffio di vento e li mulina;
pajon bambini che fan girotondo.

GLIMMERINGS

1. Collapse

I laugh when I see a baby open
its hand in the air,
thinking it's setting down an object.
I laugh no more when I observe
that to me something similar
happens, as in the emptiness
of time every nascent desire collapses,
every newborn affection.

2. Along the Way

"Let it go.... What does it matter?"
          "No stop! I want it!"
Always like that, always this war in me
between the Soul, child of heaven, and Pride,
insolent brat of the earth.

3. Ring-around-the-Roses

The bits of straw, trash in the street,
exposed to the mercy of every passerby,
also have their brief moment
of joy in the world.
A gust of wind comes and whirls them about,
they look like children playing ring-around-the-roses.

IV. Tramonto

— Di foco all'orizzonte il ciel si fascia,
lento al tramonto il sole si riduce.
— O tu che del mister sforzi le porte,
guarda! Di qua le tenebre egli lascia,
reca di là d'un nuovo dí la luce.
Ebben, chi sa? forse cosí la morte.

V. Che fai?

Batte nel cuor di tutti una campana;
ma della vita nel vario frastuono
il dolce suono
nessun ne ascolta.
Pure, talvolta,
d'un tratto giunge a noi come un'arcana
voce profonda, non udita mai.
È la lontana
chiesetta antica dell'abbandonata
nostra città...
— «Ave Maria...Ave Maria...» — Che fai,
anima sconsolata?
Lagrime amare ha chi pregar non sa...

4. Sunset

On the horizon the sky is enveloped in fire,
at dusk the sun slowly wanes.

— Oh you who strain at the gates of mystery,
look! From the darkness it leaves here
it brings forth the light of a new day.

Well, who knows? maybe death is like that....

5. What Are You Doing?

A bell rings in everyone's heart,
but in the varied commotions of life
no one hears
the soft sound.
Yet sometimes
it suddenly reaches us like a mysterious
profound voice, never heard before.
It is the distant
ancient little church abandoned
in our city...
"Ave Maria...Ave Maria...." What are you doing,
disconsolate soul?
Bitter tears for him who cannot pray.

VI. Metamorfosi

— *Vuoi darmi la manina? Ti ci metto*
un bacio. Or serra il pugno, stretto stretto;
lesta, scappa se no! —
La bambina, stupita, il pugno strinse
e il bacio, dentro, vivo, ci sentia.
Si rinchioccí presso la mamma. Illusa
e intenta, finché il sonno non la vinse,
mi guardò, mi guardò,
tenendo al petto la manina chiusa.
Nel sogno, un uccellin ne volò via.

VII. Altalena abbandonata

Legati ancora, qui, da quell'anno
questi due vecchi alberi stanno:
  il vento passa,
  agita appena
  la fune lassa
  dell'altalena...
Alle volate, or questo ramo
or l'altro dava un cigolio.
  Noi ridevamo.
Poveri vecchi! al folle brio
  di noi bambini,
tristi piegavansi, ma ressegnati.
— «*Guarda oh, che gli alberi*
ci fanno inchini!»
Li beffavamo,
noi brutti ingrati...

6. Metamorphoses

"Will you give me your hand? I'll give you
a kiss there. Now clench your fist tight, tight,
quick, it will fly away if you don't!"

The baby girl, astonished, squeezes her fist,
and the kiss, inside it, she feels to be alive.
She presses close to mamma. Credulous
and intent, until sleep overcomes her,
she watches me, watches me,
holding her closed little hand to her chest.
In her dream a bird flies out of it.

7. Abandoned Swing

Still tied here, since that year
these two old trees have been standing;
        the wind passes,
        it barely moves
        the loose rope
        of the swing....
At gusts now this or that
branch gives a creak.
        We used to laugh.
Poor old fellows! At the wild liveliness
        of us children
they bent sadly but resigned.
        "Oh look how the trees
        are bowing to us!"
        We mocked them,
        we ungrateful wretches....

VIII. Dormiveglia

Giorni oscuri, giorni stanchi!
tace l'anima, stupita
nella doglia
che le viene dalla vita;
non sa piú quel che si voglia,
non sa piú quel che le manchi.
Rotte, fievoli parole
alla bocca, non pensate, vengon sole;
ed è il corpo non curato,
senza requie torturato,
che si duole.
Quante volte, quante volte udii cosí,
trasalendo, sospirare
nelle insonni notti enormi
le mie labbra aride amare:
— Meglio, sí,
meglio assai morir; ma dormi,
ora dormi.

IX. Sorpresa

Mi parea, sú da quei greppi scoscesi,
che fosser pannilini di bucato,
gli arredi, forse, d'un bambino, stesi
su questo verde tenero del prato.

Lapidi! Un cimitero abbandonato...

X. Incontro

E ancor cammino,
senza destino:
non son vicino
e né lontan.

— Buona sera, mi t'inchino,
Sono la Morte e ti porgo la man.

8. Half-Asleep

Dark days, weary days!
The soul is mute, overcome
by the pain
that comes from life.
It no longer knows what it wants,
it no longer knows what it lacks.
Only broken, feeble words,
unthought, come to the lips,
and it is the uncared for body,
tortured without peace,
that complains.
How many times, how many times have I heard all this,
starting, sighing,
in endless, sleepless nights,
my lips bitter and dry.
"Better, yes,
much better to die, but sleep,
sleep now."

9. Surprise

It seemed to me, on those steep slopes,
that they were laundered diapers,
the garb, perhaps, of a baby stretched
out on this soft green of the meadow.

Tombstones! An abandoned cemetery....

10. Meeting

And still I walk on
to no purpose.
I am not near
nor far away.

"Good evening," I bow to you,
"I am Death, and I give you my hand."

ESAME (1910)

I

Ora che dalla vita ad un ignoto
lido seren, che sia d'un nume sede,
lanciare il ponte aereo della fede
non posso piú, ne conosco piloto

al quale il tenebroso mar sia noto
su cui quel ponte ancor lancia chi crede;
ora, s'io penso che un di sotto il piede
mi mancherà la terra (e piú del vuoto

per l'anima tremar, Morte, mi fai,
che non de la tranquilla umile fossa
che il corpo accoglierà da fiori arrisa);

credo io davver che a vivere mi possa
bastar la volontà ferma e decisa
di non pensare a questo vuoto mai?

EXAMINATION (1910)

1

Now that I can no longer throw an airy
bridge of faith from life to an unknown,
peaceful shore, home maybe to a divinity,
nor do I know a guide familiar with

the tenebrous sea, who believes that such
a bridge may still be drawn, and when
I think the earth will one day vanish
from beneath my foot (and by that void

you make my soul shudder more, Death,
than the tranquil, humble grave decked
with pleasant flowers that will receive my body):

can I truly believe that to go on living
the firm and decisive resolve will suffice
me, to never think of this void?

II

No: che se d'un pensier non lo riempio
comunque, invasa, anzi ingojata pure
la vita me ne sento, e piú né cure
che non mi pajan vane, o amor che scempio

non mi paja, mi attraggono, e se a dure
prove mi spinga pur virtú d'esempio,
vuota ogni fede, come vuoto il tempio
mi sembra, e folli tutte le avventure.

Mentre una voce ascolto che mi grida:
Come vuoi tu comprendere la vita,
se non sai pensar nulla de la morte?

Tu brancoli nel bujo della sorte
cosí, perché nell'anima smarrita
un pensier della morte non ti guida.

III

E per la morte solamente luce
chiedo perciò. D'ogni nuovo portento
che la scienza per mio ben produce,
anche ammirando, poca gioja io sento...

Son beni solo per la vita. Duce
che si ritragga dal maggior cimento,
di vincer solo nei minor contento,
piú non si sa pregiar, né piú seduce.

Sbuffa in preda al demon che lo trambascia
un ferreo mostro, e dove mai m'invola
con la sua furia? M'accorcia il cammino;

e avanti, avanti, nella notte sola,
gelida, nera, mi conduce fino
all'orlo di un abisso, e lí mi lascia.

2

No, for if I do not somehow fill the void
with thought, I feel life undermined,
even engulfed, and my cares seem all
the more vain, and love seems a calamity.

Yet they draw me on, and if an example
of virtue pushes me to a hard test,
still every faith seems empty, as the temple
is empty, and all endeavors folly.

Meanwhile I hear a voice that cries out to me:
"How can you hope to comprehend life
if you are unable to think about death?

You grope in the darkness of fate
like this because in your soul astray
there is no idea of death to guide you."

3

Thus it is for of death alone that I
crave light. With every new marvel
that science produces for my good,
even as I admire I feel little joy.

They are simply aids for life. A guide
Who pulls back from the greater test
to win satisfaction only in the lesser,
I can no longer honor, or be tempted to follow.

An iron monster pants at the mercy of the demon
that makes it suffer, and where does it carry me
in its fury? It shortens my way,

and onward, onward in the solitary night,
freezing and dark, it brings me to
the edge of an abyss, and leaves me there.

IV

E da quest'orlo or io ricerco invano
il miraggio divin d'un altro mondo
nel qual mi riposavo da lontano:
tenebra orrenda, silenzio profondo.

E invan, Scïenza, m'armi tu la mano
del fulmine domato, invan giocondo
compenso m'offri di vittorie: vano
il tuo trionfo io stimo; io ti rispondo:

Domani su l'Atlantico gittare,
nuovo prodigio, un ponte tu potrai:
ma non quell'acque, non quell'acque io temo.

Una barca che salpi oltre l'estremo
lido in cui son ridotto non mi dài
per questo tenebroso ignoto mare.

V

E se in te no, ne debbo nel primiero
sentimento a cui tu troncasti l'ale
cercare io piú la luce essenzïale
che possa alfine vincere il mistero,

debbo cercarla in me? Ma è pur fatale
che l'uomo in sé scoprir non possa il vero,
ma solo ciò che da un desio sincero
inconsciamente è indotto a creder tale.

Né dalla illusion che da me spira
potrò staccar la verità, se in seno
all'esser mio l'esser comune ha sede.

La verità? Ma ell'è come un sereno
lago, uno specchio che per se non vede
e in cui se stessa ogni persona mira.

4

And from this brink I vainly seek again
the divine mirage of another world
in which from afar I once took repose:
horrible darkness, silence profound.

It's useless, Science, to put a weapon in my hand
of tamed lightning. You offer me in vain
the happy reward of your triumphs. I find
your victory empty. I reply to you:

"Tomorrow you may be able to throw
a bridge over the Atlantic, a new miracle,
but it's not those waters I fear, not those waters.

You do not give me a boat that will sail
beyond the remote shore where I am stranded,
by this shadowy, this unknown sea."

5

And if not in you, neither may I seek
the essential light any longer in the primitive
sentiment whose wings you've cut,
that might at last have conquered the mystery.

Must I then look for it in myself? But certain
it is that man cannot discover truth
in himself but only what he is induced to
believe unconsciously by a sincere desire.

Nor by the illusion that I myself inspire
will I be able to unveil the truth, if in the heart
of my being the common being has its seat.

The truth? But it is like a peaceful
lake, a mirror that itself cannot see,
and in which every person sees only himself.

VI

Né sopra o fuor de la ragione mia
a niun Potere il pensier può dar trono,
che un mio vano fantasima non sia:
però ch'io pensi sol perch'io ragiono.

Come fuori di me non vibra suono,
né vera è dei color la poesia,
ma io soltanto, io sempre, io sempre sono
che accordo e piango la mia fantasia;

cosí, se fuor di me, stretto da un gramo
bisogno, creo qualcosa, a cui la mente
mia stessa e ogn'altra cosa vo' soggetta,

me stesso inganno, miserevolmente:
giuoco con l'ombra mia che si projetta
ingrandita nel cielo e Dio la chiamo.

VII

Or come sei tu misera davvero,
anima umana, quando contro a questa
ombra tu stessa imprechi o scherno fiero
lanci o con lei, che ascolto non ti presta

né può prestarti, scherma di pensiero
eserciti. L'idea, l'idea funesta
del male, onde ti lagni in mite o altero
verso, da lei ti vien, dall'ombra infesta

della ragion tua stessa, che tu Fato
chiami, o Natura, o Dio. Ma non esiste
se il mal che in tanta ambascia pur ti tiene,

non esiste chi l'abbia creato:
è perché è, non è né mal né bene,
ogni cosa che vive o lieta o triste.

6

To no Power above or beyond my reason
can thought give sovereignty
that is not my own vain fantasy,
for it is I alone who think, I who reason.

Outside of myself no sound vibrates,
nor are the colors of poetry true,
but it is I alone, always and only I, who
harmonizes and suffers my imagination.

Thus, if pressed by a wretched necessity
outside of myself, I create something to which
my own mind and everything else are subject,

I deceive myself miserably, I play
with my own shadow, which projects itself
magnified in the heavens, and I call it God.

7

How truly wretched you are now,
human soul, when you curse the darkness
or hurl proud scorn, or, as it pays you
no heed nor is able to, engage in a duel

of thought with it. The idea, the fatal
idea of evil that you complain of
mildly or proudly, comes to you
from the noxious darkness

of your reason itself. You call it Fate,
or Nature, or God. But the evil does not
exist that keeps you in such agony

if one who created it does not exist.
It is because it is: neither evil nor good
is every thing that lives, whether happy or sad.

VIII

Nel bujo intanto, dentro al quale impreca
e piange, o prega e spera tanta gente,
voi filosofi, andate con la mente
accesa come una lanterna cieca.

E a ciascuno di voi par vada sbieca
l'altrui lanterna, e il sentier che, fidente,
ciascun s'è scelto e al quale solamente
per sé la propria un po' di lume reca,

stima la vera via della salute,
l'altrui sentier disprezza e l'altrui zelo.
Ben per voi, fioche lucciole sperdute,

che de le stelle onde la notte è viva
lo sfavillío che punge e allarga il cielo
in terra ad esser lume non arriva.

IX

Ma se l'enorme arcan che vi disvia
che indarno prima speculaste e ch'ora,
pur senza un lume che v'imponga: — Adora!
rinunziando ad indagar che sia,

siete corrivi a creder tuttavia,
non fosse già quel che ci è ignoto ancora,
ma solo inganno che non si colora,
inganno della nostra fantasia?

Noi non siam come l'albero che vive
e non si sente, a cui la pioggia, il vento,
la terra, il sol, non par che sieno cose

ch'esso non sia, cose amiche o nocive.
Invece all'uom qual realtà s'impose,
nascendo, della vita il sentimento.

8

Meanwhile in the darkness, where many people
curse and weep, or pray and hope,
you philosophers go about with your
minds lit like blind lanterns.

And to each of you the others' lanterns
seem awry, and the path that each has
confidently chosen and to which alone
he brings a bit of light for himself,

he judges to be the one true path of well-being
and disdains the paths of others, and their zeal.
Lucky for you, lost and feeble fireflies,

that the stars' glitter, which makes the night
alive and pierces and widens the heavens,
does not reach the earth as light.

9

Even if the vast mystery that leads you astray,
about which you vainly speculated and still
now imposes itself without a light — Worship! —
renouncing to question what it may be,

have you not rushed to believe nevertheless,
even if it remains unknown to us
but only a colorless deception,
a trick of our imagination?

We are not like the tree that lives
and does not feel, to which the rain, the wind,
the earth, the sun, do not seem to be things

unlike itself, things friendly or harmful.
But for man that reality is compelling,
giving birth to the feeling of life.

X

E questo è il lume che ci fa vedere,
sperduti su la terra, il male e il bene:
la vostra lanternuccia, onde a voi viene
l'immaginario bujo; esso di nere

ombre cinge il breve àmbito in cui tiene
chiuse l'anime nostre prigioniere;
e noi dobbiam quell'ombre creder vere
fin tanto ch'esso acceso si mantiene.

Ma, spento alfine a un soffio, dopo il giorno
fumoso della nostra illusione,
ci accoglierà perpetua la notte,

o resteremo ancor, senza ritorno,
alla mercé dell'essere che rotte
le vane forme avrà della ragione?

10

And this is the light that helps us see
the good and evil spread over the earth:
your puny lantern by which the fantastic
darkness comes to you. With dark shadows

it surrounds the small circle in which
our souls are held prisoners,
and we must believe those shadows real
so long as the lanterns' light continues.

But extinguished at last with a breath, after
the smoky day of our illusion,
the eternal night will receive us.

Or will we remain still, without return,
at the mercy of the Being that will have
destroyed the vain forms of reason?

Il compito

*Il mio compito è questo: di passare
per un uom malinconico e pensoso,
un pescator che non si dia riposo
nel pescar perle nere in fondo al mare.*

*Or guaj se vengo men presso la gente
a quel concetto ch'ella s'è formato
di me, se come già m'ha immaginato
dimostro di non esser veramente.*

*Spesso di molte cose, oh tanto serie!
riderei, fino a sgangherar la bocca.
Invece, pe 'l mio compito, mi tocca
di sospirar coi labbri in giú: — Miserie!...*

My Duty

My duty is this: to pass
for a melancholy and thoughtful man,
a fisherman who never rests from
fishing for black pearls in the sea's depths.

Now woe is me if I move a little less near
the people who have formed that conception
of me, if I show myself not really to be
as they have imagined me.

I might often laugh at many things — oh very
serious things! — hard enough to dislocate my jaw.
Instead, for duty's sake I must
sigh with lips pressed down: "Oh, woe!…"

Conversando (1)

Dunque la vita in fondo
stimate da lodare,
la macchina del mondo
ben congegnata, dottor mio, vi pare.
Sí, sí, non dico... Oh, specie certe scene
son fatte proprio bene.
Ho assistito a mirabili tramonti,
a incantevoli aurore,
rider queste dai monti,
quelli infoscarsi ai limiti del mare.
E che sbalzi di cuore!
Anzi talvolta quasi m'è venuto
di battere le mani.
Poi mi son trattenuto.
Sarà lo stesso, sú per giú, dimani.
Questo il difetto, a parer mio, dottore:
poca varietà... sempre le stesse
cose... — e s'annoja alfin lo spettatore.

Conversation (1)

So life seems to you
at bottom praiseworthy,
doctor, the mechanism
of the world well-contrived.
Yes, yes, I don't mean.… Oh, certain kinds of scenes
are especially well-made.
I have witnessed marvelous sunsets
and enchanting dawns,
radiant these in the mountains
and those darken at the sea's horizon.
How my heart jumped!
Or sometimes I almost
felt like applauding.
But I restrained myself.
Tomorrow it will be more or less the same.
That's the defect, in my opinion, doctor,
not much variety…always the same
things…the spectator finally gets bored.

Conversando (2)

E debbo proprio crederci: non ha
amato mai, neppure
in sogno? Che peccato!
Mai, mai... Cosí non sa
che cosa sia l'amore.
Come? che dice? il Fato?
No, via, le lasci dir soltanto a noi
codeste brutte parolacce, oscure.
Ella, cosí bellina...
Bellina, oh questo poi
lo sa! Certo, guardandosi allo specchio,
un birichin, non visto demonietto
gliel'avrà detto — piano, in un orecchio,
ed ella avrà sorriso...
No? Perché tien cosí la testa china
e verso terra il guardo cosí fiso?
Che improvviso rossore!
Piange? Oh guarda! E non sa
che cosa sia l'amore...

Sveglia

Guizzò la prima rondine dal nido
   sotto la mia grondaja,
vibrando al cielo il breve acuto strido;
e già ne strillan cento in frotta gaja.
Filan gli aerei stridi; intanto pare
   che dai tetti vicini,
salterellando, col lor cianciugliare,
bézzichin l'aria i passeri piccini.
Giú, nel cortile, ostinasi un galletto
   nel suo verso arrochito,
— Zitto, signor Dovere, ho già capito:
è ora, è ora di lasciare il letto.

Conversation (2)

And should I really believe her, she's
never been in love, not even
in her dreams? What a pity!
Never, never.... So she doesn't know
what love may be.
How come? What does she say? Fate?
No, go on, let her say those ugly,
vague words only to us.
She so pretty....
Pretty, oh she knows all about
that! To be sure, looking at herself in the mirror,
a mischievous, invisible little demon
will have spoken to her, quietly in her ear,
and she will have smiled....
No? Why then does she bend her head
and look so fixedly at the ground?
What a sudden blush!
Is she crying? Oh look at that? And she
knows nothing about love....

Wakeup Call

The first swallow darts from the nest
   under my gutter
sounding its brief shrill cry to the heavens,
and now in a joyful swarm a hundred others squawk.
Their calls fill the air. Meanwhile it seems
   that on neighboring roofs
the little sparrows hopping about
and chattering, rapidly peck the air.
Below in the courtyard a cock persists
   in his hoarse way,
"Shut up, Master Duty, I've understood.
It's time to get out of bed."

L'ULTIMO CAFFÈ

Non poter dormire,
pe' vecchi, brutto segno
di morte vicina:
vuol dire
che il congegno
vitale si scombina.

Solo
sul tetto
della vecchia casa dirimpetto
esala un fumajolo
a spire
nell'alba
umidiccia e scialba
ul lieve fumo.
Là dirimpetto
abita un buon vecchietto
che certo è in cucina
per il suo caffè.

(Vicina
la morte
a chi non può dormire.)

Curvo sul fuoco
soffia il vechietto forte;
poi la bianca tazza
solita
prepara: tre pezzetti
di zucchero, che amato
gli sa sempre il caffè.
Schizza faville il fuoco.

(Vecchietto caro,
tu forse non m'aspetti.
Tra poco
pur verrai con me.)

The Last Coffee

He can't sleep,
for the old a bad sign
of approaching death.
It means
that the vital mechanism
is breaking down.

Alone
on the roof
of the old house opposite
a chimney gives out
a wreath
of thin smoke
into the damp and pale
dawn.
There opposite
an old fellow lives
who is surely in his kitchen
for his coffee.

(Death
is near
to one who cannot sleep.)

Bent over the fire
the old fellow blows hard,
then prepares
the usual
white cup, and three cubes
of sugar, for the coffee
always tastes bitter.
Sparks fly up from the fire.

(Dear old fellow,
perhaps you don't expect me.
Soon
you will come with me.)

Su la vasta piazza
dorme ancor l'ombra bassa;
qualche mattiniero
nero
vi passa.
Languida qualche stella
dal cielo occhieggia ancora.
Salutan la novella
squallida aurora
da presso e da lontano
i galli. Eccolo: dietro
il vetro
del balcon, pian piano
ora
sorseggia il buon vecchietto
caldo il suo caffè.
Prima che tragga il sorso,
vi soffia; chiude gli occhi:
chi sa che mai ricorda!
Forse gli sciocchi
sogni di questa notte.

Venivano
da bianche tombe
lontane
tante colombe
a frotte.
Di sotto il guanciale
aguisciava una serpetta
che gli dava un morso
sul cuore
senza fargli male.

Ancora, ancora un sorso,
vecchietto, non dar retta.
Perché ti guardi attorno?
Silenzio. Batton l'ore.

In the vast square
darkness still sleeps.
Some early riser
in black
passes by.
Lazily a few stars
still peep down from the sky.
Roosters near and far
greet the new desolate
dawn. There he is behind
the window
of the balcony, slowly
now
the good old fellow sips
his hot coffee.
Before he takes a swallow
he blows. He closes his eyes,
who knows what he is remembering?
Maybe the foolish
dreams of that night.

A flock
of pigeons comes
from distant
white tombs.
From under a pillow
wriggles a snake
that bites him
on the heart
without hurting him.

Another and another swallow,
old fellow, what are you listening for?
Why are you looking around?
Silence. The clock strikes

Le cinque. Chi t'aspetta?
È giorno, vedi? è giorno
già chiaro.
Finisci il tuo caffè

(Poi, vecchietto caro,
fa' cuore,
te ne verrai con me.)

[Senza titolo]

Sperate di rimuovere ogni danno?
Credo nel vostro ardore, amici. A un grido
vostro, tutti i dolenti insorgeranno.
Non badate, vi prego, se sorrido.
Penso, d'autunno, quante foglie ho viste
levarsi a un soffio d'aria e poi pian piano
ricader lasse su la terra triste.
Ma certo, un soffio, giova; ancor che vano.
Le pagliazze, i relitti della via,
esposti alla merce di chi cammina,
sogliono anch'essi aver cosí nel mondo
il lor breve momento d'allegria;
quel soffio d'aria. Spira, li mulina.
Pajon bambini che fan girotondo.

five. Who are you waiting for?
It's day, don't you see? It's day
already light.
Finish your coffee.

(Then, dear old fellow,
take heart,
you're not coming with me.)

[Untitled]

You'd like to rid the world of all its ills?
I believe in your passion, my friends. At
a cry from you all pain will take flight.
If I smile, don't mind me, I beg you.
I think of how many leaves I've seen in autumn
fly up at a gust of wind and then very slowly
fall wearily back to the sad earth. But surely
a puff of wind does good however aimless.
The bits of straw, trash in the street,
at the mercy of all who walk there,
also dream of having their brief moment
of happiness in the world, that puff of wind.
It whirls them up. They look like children
playing ring-around-the-rosie.

Improvvisi

I

Chi dice che il tempo passa?
Passa il tempo che non è nulla.
Io ti vedo, Maria Lembo,
come tu eri da fanciulla,
col tuo abito nuovo di faglia,
a righine bianche e blu;
sotto l'ali e le ghirlande
di quel tuo grande cappello di paglia,
vedi, il tempo non passa piú.

M'hanno detto che sei morta;
ma eri vecchia e poco importa;
sono anch'io vecchio, Maria,
ma ora son giovine con te,
al Casino Valadier,
sulla terrazza che guarda Roma;
vuoi sapere dov'è Tordinona,
Tordinona che piú non c'è:
eccola, dico, non temere
che la zia
ti veda con me.

II

Vivo del sogno di un'ombra nell'acqua:
ombra di rame verdi, di case
giú capovolte, e di nuovo nuvole… e tremola
tutto: lo spigolo bianco d'un muro
nel cielo azzurro abbagliante, una corda
che l'attraversa, un fanale e il tronco
nero d'un albero, tagliato a mezzo
  da un foglio giallo
  di carta che galleggia…

Impromptus

1

Who says that time passes?
The passing of time is nothing at all.
I see you, Maria Lembo,
as when you were a little girl,
in your new silk dress
with blue and white stripes,
under the wide brim and
garlands of your big straw hat.
You see, time doesn't ever pass.

They've told me that you're dead,
but you were old and it doesn't matter.
I, too, am old, Maria,
but now I'm young with you,
at the Casino Valadier,
on the terrace looking over Rome.
You want to know where Tordinona is,
Tordinona that exists no more.
There it is, I say, don't be afraid
that your aunt
will see you with me.

2

I live in the dream of a shadow in water,
shadow of a green branch, of houses
upside down, and of new clouds…and it all
trembles, the white corner of a wall
in the dazzling blue of the sky, a cord
that runs across it, a street lamp, and the black
trunk of a tree, cut in half
  by a sheet of yellow
  paper floating.…

*Ombra nell'acqua — liquida città...
luminoso tremore, vastità
il cielo chiaro, verde verde verde
di foglie — tutto par che vada e sta
e vive e non lo sa;
non lo sa l'acqua, non lo sanno gli alberi,
non lo sa il cielo né le case... Solo
un pover'uomo lo sa, che va
lungo l'argine triste
del canale.*

Shadow in the water — liquid city…
bright trembling, immensity
of clear sky, green green green
of leaves — everything seems to move and be still
and alive and doesn't know it.
The water does not know, nor do the trees,
nor the sky, nor the houses.… Only
a poor man knows it, who walks
along the sad bank
of the canal.

Notes

All the poems in this book are printed in the order of their appearance in *Tutte le poesie*, edited by Manlio Lo Vecchio-Musti (Mondadori, 1982). All the texts are derived from the same source.

Page
1   *Mal giocondo* (Palermo: [S.N.], 1889). The poems of *Mal giocondo* are organized into five groups: "Romanzi," "Allegre," "Intermezzo lieto," "Momentanee," and "Triste." These titles help to give the appearance of order, but they actually indicate very little about the themes or subjects of the groups, so we have retained the Italian titles even for the English translations.
    The title "Mal giocondo" is virtually untranslatable. "Mal" means bad or badly; "giocondo" means gay or jolly. Evidently the phrase is meant to suggest a mixture of moods or outlooks. I have followed the lead of Alastair Hamilton, translator of Giudice's biography of Pirandello. (Gaspare Giudice, *Luigi Pirandello* [Turin: UTET, 1963], translated by Alastair Hamilton as *Pirandello: A Biography* [London: Oxford University Press, 1975]).

4   "Allegre I": Zeus was known as a cloud-gatherer, but Pirandello seems to be thinking of Hermes here, who stole cattle from the herd belonging to Apollo.

6   "Intermezzo lieto I": Pirandello, who read French writers all his life, might well have been influenced by Baudelaire's famous title. Baudelaire died in the year Pirandello was born.

21 Appendix to *Pasqua di Gea* (Milan: Libreria editrice Galli, 1891). Gea or Gaia was the earth-goddess, source of all life. The appendix is an addition and conclusion to a longer sequence of similar poems published in 1891. They were dedicated to Jenny Schulz-Lander, Pirandello's lover during the last year of his stay in Bonn.

27   *Elegie renane* (Rome: Tipografia dell'unione coop editrice, 1895). Pirandello uses the term "elegies" to denote a verse form traceable to classical Greece and Rome. Usually made of couplets of uneven length, it may serve a variety of narrative or meditative purposes, not necessarily related to death or mourning. Another well-known modern example, not in couplets, is Rilke's *Duino Elegies*. The passage included here is of special interest because it is plainly autobiographical: it depicts Pirandello's relationship with Jenny Schulz-Lander and frankly reveals his ambivalence concerning this intimacy.

33   *Zampogna* (Rome: Società editrice Dante Aligheri, 1901). These poems have a distinctive quality not found elsewhere in Pirandello's poetry (or prose for that matter), namely a precise and delicate rendering of natural images. He never quite forgot that, although a bookworm, he was brought up in the country, and the "Zampogna" are evidently a concentrated and deliberate exploitation of a store of memories.

47   "Summer Storm, 2." Tufa is a variety of limestone, says Wikipedia, "formed by the precipitation of carbonate minerals from ambient temperature water bodies." It is found in many parts of Italy.

65   *Fuori di chiave* (Genoa: Formiggini, 1912). *Fuori di chiave* was Pirandello's last volume of poetry, published when he was 45 years old. Many poems written before and after were not collected and are gathered in chronological order as "Poesie varie" in the Mondadori volume of "Tutte le poesie." The date of this volume makes it unmistakeably clear that Pirandello's poems were not mere "apprentice" work as has sometimes been asserted.

67   "Prelude: Orchestral." This poem seems to be an unusual and highly uncharacteristic exercise in self-mockery. The lady in the contrabass may be Pirandello's cousin Lina to whom he was engaged for several years. Having gained her affection, he lost interest in her, and the dissolution of the engagement must have involved some extraordinary scenes. What is known of this episode — not very much — is to be found in the second chapter of Giudice's biography.

67   "Of Departure" accompanies the confusion and disorder of the "Prelude" as a dream of escape. This is a theme referred to several times by Pirandello: the quest at sea for a land of

peace and serenity, dreamt of but always elusive.

71 "Entrance." The stories of Prometheus and Pandora are rather complex. Following Robert Graves' summary, suffice it to say that Prometheus was punished by Zeus for his favors to humanity (whom he had created) by having his liver torn out by a vulture every day. And Pandora, made of clay and very beautiful, though intended for Prometheus, was married by his brother, Epimetheus. She opened the box entrusted to his brother by Prometheus and thus loosed all the causes of suffering upon the world. Making her the doorkeeper to life is Pirandello's invention.

91 "Melbthal." The exquisite detail of this story has the effect of making it seem the record of an actual event. Yet the biographical material for Pirandello's life makes no mention of Else. She is not present in Giudice's authoritative biography or Camilleri's more informal one. Pirandello's own autobiographical poem "Convegno" *(Meeting)* which brings together his earlier selves accompanied by their lovers gives Jenny a prominent place, but Else is not present.

Still, a second poem exists, its publication dated 1898, that raises doubts. It, too, is titled "Melbthal," and it too is addressed to Else. It is not a very demonstrative poem, but its implication seems clear:

Ascolta come tentano gli uccelli
coi primi trilli il fresco aer d'aprile.
……
Odi, Else,
………
L'un chiama l'altro e la risposta aspetta:
tempo è di fabbricare i nuovi nidi.

Listen how the birds test the fresh
April air with their early songs.
……
Do you hear, Else.
……
One calls the other and waits for an answer:
it's time to build the new nests.

Was Else real or imagined?

117 "Reading History." Vannozza (1442–1518) was mistress of Rodrigo Borgia, who became Pope Alexander VI in 1492. She was the mother of four of his children, who included the famous and oft-married Lucrezia Borgia.
"Canal." Carlo Canale of Mantua, who managed to serve both the Gonzaga and Borgia families, the latter especially as designated husband to Vannozza. He preserved and saw published the manuscript of Politian's *Orfeo*.
"Poliziano." Or sometimes "Politian" in English, the author of *Orfeo*. He was immensely talented, a poet in Greek and Latin, but he asserted his influence in support of the Tuscan dialect as capable of high literary expression.

123 "Poesie Varie." (Various Poems, Uncollected).
After 1912 Pirandello published no more books of poetry, but he continued to write poems, to publish them in journals, and to revise many of the earlier versions. They were gathered by the editor Manlio Lo Vecchio Musti from many sources and first published together in Volume VI of Pirandello's Collected Works (Mondadori, 1960).

124 "Il Globo" as "Globo," from *Nazione letteraria*, June 1893; reprinted in *La riviera ligure*, August 1905.

126 "Lieta" from *Folchetto* 4, 25 March 1894, reprinted in *Nuova antologia*, 1 March 1907.

130 "Amor sincero" from *Folchetto* 4.240, 31 August 1894.

132 "Notte insonne" from *La lettura*, November 1901.

138 "La Via" with the subtitle "Labirinto. — Intermezzo," from *Gazzetta letteraria*, 12 January 1895.

142 "Alba" from *Natura ed arte* 5.13, June, with the indication Labirinto, Lib. I, Tarlo antico.

146 "Esame (1895)" from *Roma letteraria* 3.19.10, with the indication Labirinto, Lib. IV, "Auspicî."

148 "Approdo" from *La Critica*, edited by Gino Monaldi, 29 October 1895, reprinted in *Noi e il mondo*, 1 January 1914.

150 "Torna, Gesú" from *La Critica*, edited by Gino Monaldi, 28 December 1895.

154 "Esame (1896)" from *Roma letteraria* 4.16, 25 August 1896, with the indication Labirinto, Lib. I, Tarlo antico.

156 "L'abbandono" from *Marzocco*, 18 June 1899, and from *Noi e il mondo*, 1 January 1914.

164 "Primo rintocco" from *La riviera ligure* 36, February 1902.

168 "Esame (1906)" from *Nuova antologia*, 1 September 1906.

170 "Esame (1906) 3". The language of this piece is almost certainly intended to recall the opening lines of Dante's *Inferno*. The translation, therefore, echoes several of the best known translations of the "Inferno's" beginninng: see those by John Ciardi, Robert Durling, and Jean and Robert Hollander.

174 "Tenui luci improvvise" from *La riviera ligure* 57, February 1904.

182 "Esame (1910)" from *Nuova antologia*, 16 August 1910.

194 "Il compito" from *Nuova antologia*, 16 August 1910.

196 "Conversando" from *Nuova antologia*, 16 August 1910.

198 "Sveglia" from *Nuova antologia*, 16 August 1910.

200 "L'ultimo caffé," published in *La riviera ligure* 6, June 1912, then revised. This text is from the author's papers, typewritten copy with handwritten notes.

   The speaker of this poem evidently is the same one who appears in the tenth poem of "Glimmerings" (p. 181), namely Death.

207 "Impromtus." These two poems are from *Nuova antologia*, 1 January 1934, edited by Corrado Alvaro, and dated approximately 1932–33. They were reprinted after the author's death in *L'almanacco letteraria* (Milan: Bompiani, 1938).

   "Casino Valadier" is an early nineteenth-cenury building on the Pincian hill famous for its view of Rome from the terrace. Still a fashionable restaurant and open-air café.

   "Tordinona." There is still a Via Tordinona in Rome, but the district, as the poem points out, was long ago torn down and rebuilt.

⊙ ⊙ ⊙

APPENDIX 1

FROM *ARTE E COSCIENZA D'OGGI*
(ART AND CONSCIOUSNESS IN OUR TIME)
1893

II

...Modern philosophy has aimed to explain the universe as a living machine and has done its best to clarify the knowledge we have of it. And then it has gone on to determine humanity's place in nature, to interpret life, and to deduce its purposes.

The truth certainly was never a deceiver. Deception was always the result of imagining too much. Nevertheless, it's a sad place that science has assigned to us in nature, at least in contrast with the one we imagined for ourselves in earlier times. A humorist poet might find in this a subject for some songs. Once upon a time the earth was the umbilicus of a boundless creation. The entire sky, the sun, the stars, turned around it continually, as if to offer it a spectacle and make night and day for it. All respectable human beings, hands clasped on their stomachs, could happily enjoy this immense spectacle and in their hearts praise the Lord God who had created so many beautiful things for their sake, as well as cattle for their meat, and grapes for wine, and the horse for its strong back, and so forth and so on. In that time the moon rose slowly over a restless sea, the sea bore it up like a great egg yolk, and respectable people clapped their hands and exclaimed, "Yes, this scene is well-done!"

Then, when they finally died, heaven and hell were set in motion. Angels and devils disputed their souls, as one reads even in a poem by Vincenzo Monti, and the soul saved itself with the angels. Where? It's not precisely known, but one climbed up high, high, to the kingdom of the heavens, in a region unknown to modern astronomy called Paradise, created by God for god alone and the righteous. And there one enjoyed oneself and obtained the reward and compensation for long sufferings here below. Suffering? But to suffer on earth was less than nothing! It was rather an offering for the sake of another life. The true life was death. And there had earlier been a time when the earth was considered the homeland of gods, and certain people ranged over it far and wide believing themselves demi-gods, armed and swathed in ample togas. Oh, what times those were, and how one could strut about dressed up like a Greek of Pericles' century or a Roman in the brilliance of the Republic. *Civis romanus sum!* (I am a citizen of Rome!) and Rome was *caput mundi* (head of the world). And to the Sun, which was a god, and to the Moon, which was a goddess of many names, Horace, priest of them both, sang that nothing greater had ever been seen, that nothing greater would ever be seen!

As for the philosophers, they have been, are, and always will be great sluggards. I willingly apply to them the brutal saying that an Austrian emperor used to repeat concerning poets: "The poets are a family of invalids who by profession spread a sick feeling among the people." And I would unhesitatingly begin by kicking Plato himself out of his ideal republic.

We all know, unfortunately, to what they have reduced the earth! An astral atom, immeasurably small, a most ordinary little top thrown out one fine day from the sun and spinning around it in space on an immutable course. What has the individual become? What has this microcosm, this king of the universe become? Alas, poor king! Don't you see King Lear leap up before you armed with a broom in all his tragic comicality? Why is he raving? There was once a proud castle, a marvelous castle built on a red cloud, a cloud that seemed like flame. That castle was his palace, and the wind carried it away. The sun went down, and the cloud changed. It became livid and then little by little black. Finally it broke down into water, and those droplets looked like tears. Then from that rain certain sad, ashen grass sprang up on a plain, bristly with thorns. The king gathered them up. With his bloody hands he made himself a crown. Then he began to walk solemnly among a mass of tadpoles and froglets who jump around him on all sides croaking in chorus: the Man is all mud! And now, as if he did not feel himself small enough, here are certain phantoms of his frightened mind made into persons and coming toward him. They spread a coat under his feet and raise him up to fly. And the poor fellow, lost in space without a destination, asks in anguish:

> Is it true? that little
> blue globe immersed in the ether
> to which a smaller, similar disc draws near
> that lights up our nights, is that our
> paradise? And the walls, where are they?
> Where the gatekeepers?

He climbs on and on and ends by completely losing the earth in the limitless immensity of the skies. He does not find God up there, nor has he recovered the earth down here as he imagined it until now. He sees its rottenness but not its poverty, since his spirit has been able to soar and embrace so much space. In vain he meets a philosopher with the air of a priest of a new, very rational cult, who preaches to him that after all the earth was very well able to express itself to humanity about the terrifying void, emptied of gods, that surrounds it, and to be considered as existing in and for itself, the little homeland of little beings, all bent upon procuring such happiness as was possible, no longer relying on heaven, but on ideals belonging to earth without asking for anything else. Humanity declaiming again with solemn gestures and majestic posturing that tirade of proud rhetoric:

Omnes homines, qui sese student... (All beings, who desire to distinguish themselves... Sallust), we are not heard imitating the wise cattle, for whom the only truth that exists is the grass that grows under their chins. And then from this little pedestal of the earth, we set about, tragic and shaggy-haired, desperately to demand accounting and reason from nature of all that it has made. And here, between us and the new priesthood, was initiated one of the most comic disputes ever recorded in the centuries-old annals of the earth. It seems that humanity itself must have come from *monkeys*, and at this humanity was disdainfully indignant. Who if not God had created all things? "No one," we were told, the universe is explained as a natural formation, as evolutionary; "and you cannot understand it if you do not restore in yourself the correspondence between intellect and the real." And what is the real? "It is what is!" And what do you know about what is, if you don't even know how your ideas are formed, in what way they are derived from the breakdown of substances, or by what means a chemical process is transmuted into the knowledge of things? We can have no knowledge, no precise idea, about life, but only a feeling that is changeable and various. A feeling! Feeling belongs to poetry, not to science.... What is nature? "A symbol of mechanical groupings which, changing their relations continually, ascend to vast forms of motion, each bringing its own law." If you investigate this law and the eternal necessity that governs the real, you will go on to ask certain foolish questions, the product of human pride that wishes to place itself at the center of the universe. You are impertinent lunatics! Where do we come from? Where are we going? What do we await here in the uncertainty of fate? For what purpose do I live? But life has no purpose. It has causes that determine it, since we, too, like all visible creation, are subject to the universal laws of causality. "Life is the necessary result of the functioning of nature's mechanical forces in accordance with their laws, and it includes within itself a certain quantity of pleasures and of pains. The first consists in the satisfaction of our instincts, and the other in vain longings to be able to satisfy them." But each person would like to satisfy one's own particular instincts. Who will cultivate them? Who will govern them? What will the norms of conduct be? Which actions will be regarded as good and which bad, which just or unjust? Here is the real knot. Here the most essential part of the problem....

III

As for the old-timers, you've understood them: they declare that a great deal of science has passed before them with little or no effect on souls, leaving them indifferent and turned to God. Others, stubborn in asking the reason of everything and especially of those facts the causes of which are quite inaccessible to us, seeing that their researches and investigations are getting nowhere, from the believers that they were, are reduced to accepting a vulgar phenomenology.

The young make an even sadder spectacle.... An extraordinary confusion rules in their heads and consciousness. In this interior mirror are reflected the most disparate figures, all however in attitudes of disarray, as if weighed down with insupportable burdens, and each with a different view of things. Whom to listen to, whom to cling to? The persistence of one opinion wins for a time everyone else's agreement, and we abandon ourselves to it with the sickly impulsiveness of those who want to find safety and don't know where to go. At the same time almost all of us flaunt our disdain for every traditional opinion.... We feign indifference with a certain discreet arrogance for everything we don't know and that at bottom we want to know, and we feel ourselves having gone astray, or rather lost in an immense blind labyrinth surrounded entirely by an impenetrable mystery. There are many ways to go. Which one is right? People are rushing here and there, and each one gives itself the air of understanding something, so much so that at certain times some one of us stops struck by a serious doubt and asks oneself: "Can I be the only one who understands nothing?" Eh, yes, certain people really make one wonder. It's hard to believe, seeing them, that they're not fully convinced that we must remain beasts in order to keep going on at least in peace! And perhaps they're not wrong. Meanwhile, which way to go? What guiding rule to follow? No one dares to persist in a path to its end, we stop half way, we want to look back to see the others, and doubt rises to our lips. What if I'm wrong? Maybe over there the way out is found. And we set out in another direction. There are always a few people who come along behind us like so many bodyguards, who imitate our actions, repeat our words, do whatever we do.

The old norms broken down, new ones not yet achieved or well-defined. It's natural that the concept of relativism in everything should be so widespread among us as to cause the loss of all ability to judge. The field is open to all suppositions. Intellect has acquired an extraordinary mobility. No one is in a position to establish a point of view that is strong and unshakable. Abstract terms have lost their value, lacking common meanings that make them comprehensible.

Never, I think, has our life been ethically and esthetically so fragmented. Cut loose, without any principle of doctrine and faith, our thoughts whirl among restless fates that hover like clouds above a ruin. From this, in my opinion, comes most of our intellectual malaise. We await, unfortunately in vain, for someone who will emerge and announce to us the new word. And meanwhile we turn to this or that prophet who, ranting loudly, promises oceans and mountains and naturally produces nothing. Whence the incalculable outpouring of the most bizarre rubbish in this international carnival of folly: castles of sand that are demolished at the least breath of wind; sudden glories that last for a day like the newspapers; fashions, schools, gangs, fortunes swept away and lost in a moment. Yesterday realism and naturalism, today symbolism and mysticism, tomorrow who knows what. Have you seen an opera by Wagner? Yesterday they said it was the music of lunatics. Today they say it's sublime. It's not well understood. But who can tell what profound philosophy it contains. What if it finally contains the meaning of life? And now everyone is on the trail of Wagnerism, in search of this meaning of life. Have you seen a play of Ibsen's? What does he want of us, this Norwegian? No one sees it clearly. But it's enough for someone to appear momentarily incomprehensible in order to be instantly surrounded by the swarm of tireless seekers, overwhelmed — allow me the vulgar image — like a wad of spit by flies.

An esthetic theory of knowledge has even been arrived at: knowledge as an end in itself. To know for the sake of knowing, not to know for action, that is, to study life, not live it. Art consists in the precise rendering of thoughts, of the slightest and most hidden unfolding of feelings, of all the reasons and nuances of every sensation: to sense and breathe the perfume of life, and to go beyond it. The soul is thus in constant motion: a curious bee. This is modern dilettantism, and its adherents wish to see Stendhal as their chief.

There is another expression of contemporary debility, the characteristic signs of which are egotism, moral exhaustion, lack of courage in the face of adversity, pessimism, nausea, self-disgust, indolence, lack of will, inclination to daydream, emotional excitability, mania for imitation, and boundless self-esteem. This one lies down, or rather stretches out, in a concept of fatal determinism.

Now think a little of those others who, in order to find, as they say, an escape however momentary, from complete moral shipwreck, have rigidly enclosed themselves in themselves, shedding as much as possible every tie and reducing little by little their needs and aspirations. After a while, naturally, they began to feel estranged from life, uninterested and lacking curiosity. There emerged also among them an invincible disgust for all the daily vulgarity, and from a cold and dispassionate observation of the feelings and behavior of others, more or less always the same ones, an oppressive boredom. "Ah, life!" they exclaim: an empty and useless game of actions and words! "And then, and then?" is the insistently repeated question. Always and everywhere the same things! For so little, then, so much effort! And they wait in vain for something to happen — as long as it's new and extraordinary — that will finally rouse and interest them. Now they become aware that the supposed liberation was only supercilious and painful renunciation, and that calm, only solitary, empty, silent. The spectacle of the world gives them the image of a hungry machine to which someone (we don't know why or how) has imparted motion, and to which without let up all beings are thrown, immolated victims feeding the great fire. They would like, if possible, to have witnessed the spectacle of this universal combustion without burning, like so many brands far from the fire among the cold ashes. But now they feel the cold of these ashes penetrate their souls, and they are profoundly depressed. After all, they no longer know how to throw themselves into the fire, or they would like at least to see clearly beforehand a purpose for doing so.

> "To burn, why?"
> "To live!"
> "And to live, why?"

Pale cares come to knock at the gates of their sad and lonely dream, weighed down by a tangle of chains. "Open up! The world demands it of you. The present moment doesn't allow a solitary good." And bitter needs knock, still more enslaved than the cares: "Open up, you too must come down to drag your chains!..."

Give voice again to all the generous figures of history who fought for a human ideal, and achieving it naturally thought they had at last provided a stable basis for life. Go back to the past, search out and recall all those generous ones who have brought about the progress of humanity. But life does not know peace, as the sea does not know peace. And history will appear to you like that Dantean whirlwind of souls all prey to a struggle that has no rest....

One is drawn to compare this moment of life to some other dark time traversed by humanity, even to see the decline not only of an entire religious, political, and philosophical idea, but the twilight of peoples: not merely a *fin de siècle* but a *fin de race*.

And all this, while science every day employs its strengths to new and marvelous purposes by means of nature, and the comforts of life have so increased that everyone must find this brief residence on earth easy and enjoyable. Can't we then look around ourselves more and take account of the wonders humanity has accomplished in this day and age? Are there then no miracles either for the eyes or for the soul?...

Some would like art to become the echo or mouthpiece of the democratic tendency that they think presently runs through the modern consciousness. Others would like art to sing the praises of science's triumphs, and they end up proposing a great number of extraordinary subjects for the modern lyre.

That art may be, so to speak, the pulse of life, that it may follow and reflect every movement of life, are obvious and uncontested propositions. Considering the various hints given by the times, the tendency of contemporary works and thought, what will the art of tomorrow be like? As critics we can respond very well to this question or direct it to others. Bad news to us, however, if we direct it to art, if we undertake, that is, to create art according to a rule or argument, when it ought to be born spontaneously from feeling.

I do not know if modern consciousness is truly as democratic and scientific as it is commonly said to be. There are certain abstract affirmations that I don't understand. To me modern consciousness conveys the image of an anguished dream, a nocturnal battle, populated by flitting ghosts, sad or threatening, in which a thousand banners are raised for a moment and immediately disappear, and the contending parties are confused and commingled, each one fighting for itself, defending itself against friend or enemy. And there is a continual clash of discordant voices, a continual agitation. Everything appears trembling and wobbling. Nor do I believe in the calm confidence of certain serene individuals. What will tomorrow bring? We are surely on the eve of an enormous event. And perhaps now, too, the genius will emerge who, confronting with his or her soul the approaching storm and the sea that will overflow its banks and engulf the ruins, will create the unique and timeless book, just as was done in former times

Appendix 2

AN AUTOBIOGRAPHICAL LETTER (1914)

I was born in Sicily, to be exact in a country house near Girgenti, on the 28th of June 1867. I came to Rome for the first time in 1886 and stayed for two years. In October of 1888, I left for Germany and remained there for two and a half years, that is, until April, 1891. I took a degree in Letters and Philosophy at the University of Bonn. In 1891, I returned to Rome and have stayed there ever since. For fifteen years I have, unfortunately, taught Stylistics[1] at the Women's Faculty of Education *(Istituto di Magistero)*. I say "unfortunately" not only because teaching is a heavy burden for me, but because my most ardent hope would be to withdraw to the country in order to work.

In Rome I live secluded as much as possible. I don't go out except for a few hours in the evening to get some exercise, accompanied as it may happen, by a friend: Giustino Ferri or Ugo Fleres.

I rarely go to the theater. At ten in the evening I am in bed. I get up early and regularly work until noon. After lunch I usually go back to my desk at 2:30 and stay until 5:30, but after the morning hours I do no more writing except for some urgent necessity, but I read or study. In the evening after dinner, I stay and talk for a while with my family. I read

---

1. Stylistics. Defined by the *Enciclopedia Zanichelli* as the "study of the practices and procedures characteristic of a literary genre in a given epoch or of a particular author. In this sense it corresponds to ancient rhetoric, with the difference that its approach is exclusively descriptive and not prescriptive." Perhaps the courses taught by Pirandello resembled what in American universities is often called Composition.

the headlines of articles and columns in some newspaper, and to bed.

As you see, there's nothing in my life that deserves special attention. All of it is interior, in my work and in my thoughts which...are not cheerful.

I think that life is a very sad farce, because we have in ourselves, despite being unable to know how, or why, or from whom, a necessity to deceive ourselves continuously with the spontaneous creation of a reality (one for each and never the same for all), which little by little we discover to be vain and illusory.

Whoever has understood this game never again succeeds in deceiving himself. But whoever cannot deceive himself never again has an appetite for life or can take pleasure in it. That's the way it is.

My art is full of bitter compassion for all those who deceive themselves, but this compassion cannot but be followed by fierce scorn for the destiny that condemns mankind to deceit.

This in brief is the reason for the bitterness of my art, and also of my life.

The books. — My first book was a collection of poems, *Mal giocondo* (Troubled Joy), published before my departure for Germany. I note this fact because it has been said that my "humorism" *(umorismo)* originated during my stay in Germany. That is not true. In the first collection of poems more than half were starkly "humoristic," and at that time I did not even know what "humorism"was....[2]

---

2. What does Pirandello mean when he talks about "umorismo"? This was an important idea to him, and he published a monograph in the effort to explain it. It's no real help to translate the word into an English neologism like "humorism," a word that seems to refer to the making of jokes.

For an authoritative brief definition, a short paragraph will be quoted from an excellent book by Anthony Caputi, *Pirandello and the Crisis of Modern Cosnsciousness* (Urbana: University of Illinois Press, 1988).

The example of the old woman is borrowed from Pirandello himself.

Instead I wrote *Easter in Gea* (Pasqua di Gea) in Germany, a long poem of spring, loosely rhymed in seven-syllable verse, and in no way "humoristic." And also the *Elegie rename (Rhenish Elegies)*.

Back in Rome, I translated Goethe's *Elegie romane (Roman Elegies)*.

Until the end of 1892, it did not seem to me possible to write otherwise than in verse. I owe it to Luigi Capuana who pushed me to try narrative art in prose. (I say "narrative art in prose" because until very recently I had in my drawer the manuscript of a long narrative in verse, a poem on the Archdevil Belfagor, it too composed before my going to Germany, and it too humoristic.)

My first experiment in prose narrative was the novel *L'esclusa (The Outcast)*, 1901, published by Treves, and later edited and corrected. The first collection of stories, *Amori senza amore (Lovers without Love)* came out in 1894.

(From this point on the letter is nothing but a record of publications.)

> Essentially the monograph deals with the way things in Pirandello's conception of that term are shaped and organized within the consciousness and at the same time are mediated by a humoristic way of seeing. This mode of perception, or power of reflection, as he frequently called it, involves a kind of x-ray vision that provides both positive and negative images simultaneously. We see the old lady made ridiculous by her excessive makeup, and we laugh because she is trying so hard to appear a young lady. But at the same time we see that she suffers with this mask because she wears it to hold the love of her much younger husband. *Umorismo* is this way of treating the image of the woman. More a way by which many faculties collaborate than a single faculty, it was for Pirandello the dominant modality for modern consciousness.

In a new translation of *Sei Personaggi (Six Characters in Search of an Author,* trans. by Martha Witt and Mary Ann Frese Witt [New York: Italica Press, 2013], p. 20, n. 3), Mary Ann Frese Witt writes, "Pirandello uses the word *umoristico* to describe the mixed feelings of laughter and sympathy, or comic and tragic modes, that a character may invoke. See also her introduction at pp. xv–xvi.

CHRONOLOGY

1867   Luigi Pirandello was born June 28 at a family homestead near Agrigento, famously named Cavasu, the Sicilian word for Chaos. His father, Stefano, was a well-off sulfur merchant, a former campaigner in Garibaldi's army. His mother, Caterina Ricci Gramitto, came from the same milieu. She had already given birth to a young daughter, Rosalina, and an earlier child who died in infancy.

1870s   Luigi was entered into commercial school by his father, but he was strongly drawn to the classical curriculum of the *ginnasio*, took and passed the entrance exam, and won his father's permission to attend.

1882–88   His family moved to Palermo where Pirandello completed his *ginnasio* studies. In 1886 he enrolled in the Faculty of Letters at the University but transferred to Rome the following year.

1889   He published his first book in Palermo, poems entitled *Mal giocondo* (Troubled Joy). Leaving Rome after arousing the ire of the Dean of the Faculty of Letters, he enrolled in the University of Bonn.

1891   He took a degree in Romance philology, writing a dissertation, in German, on the dialect of Agrigento. During the last year of his stay in Bonn, he had an affair with a bold and handsome girl, Jenny Schulz-Lander. He dedicated his second book to her: *Pasqua di Gea* (Easter in Gea).

1892   Settled in Rome and supported by his father, he began a furiously productive literary career.

1894   Marriage to Maria Antonietta Portulano by arrangement between their two fathers. By character and temperament they were utterly unsuited. Her innocence had been obsessively guarded by her family. She had no literary or intellectual interests. After giving birth to three children, her mental health deteriorated. She was cared for at home

	until 1919, when she was placed in a nursing home. She lived until 1959.
1895	He published *Elegie Renane* (Rhenish Elegies).
1901	*Zampogna* (Bagpipes) published.
1903	His father's sulphur mine ruined by flood, Pirandello began to write for money and took a job teaching at the Magistero, the teacher-training faculty for women. He held this job for many years while carrying on his literary work. In 1904 he brought out in serialized form his most successful and admired novel, *Il fu Mattia Pascal (The Late Mattia Pascal)*.
1908–15	A very active period of literary work: novels, stories, poetry.
1912	His last book of poems published: *Fuori di chiave* (Offkey).
1915–20	During this period the stage became Pirandello's principal sphere of activity.
1921	The first production of *Sei personaggi in cerca d'autore (Six Characters in Search of an Author)*, the play that made Pirandello internationally famous.
1924	He hired for a new theater, of which he was manager and director, a beautiful young actress named Marta Abba. He was in love with her to the end of his life. She became his muse as well as his leading lady. She called him "Maestro." The relationship seems not to have become more intimate than that,
	During the '20s and '30s Pirandello was sympathetic to the Fascist movement, though never an active campaigner. He thought Mussolini might finance a new national theater but was disappointed in that hope.
1934	Pirandello was awarded the Nobel Prize for Literature.
1936	He died in Rome on December 10th, 69 years old. Eventually he was buried at his birthplace, Chaos.

☉ ☉ ☉

Index of First Lines — Italian

Accendi il lume nella stanza triste	162
Al violin trillante una sua brava	66
All'ingresso della vita	70
Alla porta del sogno in cui, riparo	134
Appena qualche foglia, ad ora ad ora	48
Batte nel cuor di tutti una campana	176
Casa romita in mezzo a la natia	58
Che hai fatto? Dimmi, forse perché	106
Che m'avviene?	126
Che so di me? So quel che il tempo vuole	168
Chi dice che il tempo passa?	206
Chi mai vorrà comprare le mie nuvole?	4
Concepito ho il grave dubbio	138
Concreta, esprimi il tuo desio: che vuoi?	146
Dalla branda, sospesa tra due rami	52
Del forestier che ancora il sol della patria ha negli occhi	28
Di foco all'orizzonte il ciel si fascia	176
Dunque la vita in fondo	196
E al fine, eccomi in porto. Ancor mi resta	148
E ancor cammino	180
E da quest'orlo or io ricerco invano	186
E debbo proprio crederci: non ha	198
E le parlai cosí, piú d'una volta	156
E per la morte solamente luce	184
E questo è il lume che ci fa vedere	192
E se in te no, ne debbo nel primiero	186
E sei vivo anche tu, come son io	108
Ecco, a un mandorlo appende	34
Ecco il globo: una palla di cartone	124
Ecco la folla. — Chierici e beoni,	12
Ella ciarlava molto	92
Esausta, muta, sotto l'affocato	54
Eterno eterno eterno!	22
Eterno immenso e vario	18
Facciam conto una vettura	80
Facile a dire, sceglersi una via!	138

Forse perché lo guardo da una faccia	154
Fuggono i giorni miei sí come accolti	8
Giorni oscuri, giorni stanchi!	180
Gira, gira…Nello spazio	76
Gli alberetti di mandorlo, piccini	40
Godi, o mia carne, fino a che perdura	12
Guizzò la prima rondine dal nido	198
Il bosco parea fatto	90
Il gelso? Non c'è piú. C'è solo il masso	58
Il mio compito è questo: di passare	194
Il paese che un dí sognai, del mondo	2
Intenderà, pensavo: oggi o dimani	156
Io fui tratto con urti violenti	170
Io mi sento guardato da le stelle	132
Io sono come l'albero che aspetta	62
Io vorrei che le donne graziose	130
L'anima or segue nella notte il fiume	136
La memoranda notte è ormai vicina	150
La mia vicina, sul mattin d'aprile	96
Lascia… Che importa?	174
Le pagliuzze, i relitti della via	174
Legati ancora, qui, da quell'anno	178
Levo ogni tanto dal guancial la testa	164
Lunga speranza e desiderii brevi…	130
Ma la Terra, se non bella	76
Ma se l'enorme arcan che vi disvia	190
Mettiti a camminare	74
Mi parea, sú da quei greppi scoscesi	180
Mi trovo qui per caso, di passaggio	138
Navi ho veduto per lontani mari	170
Naviga lenta pe i silenzi arcani	6
Né sopra o fuor de la ragione mia	188
Nel bujo intanto, dentro al quale impreca	190
No: che se d'un pensier non lo riempio	184
Non poter dormire	200
Non siam fatti per capire	78
O castagni del bosco, un altro cielo	38
O vecchia Terra, è vero, e me ne pento	120
Ogni attimo che fugge m'ammaestra	8
Or come sei tu misera davvero	188
Ora che ai cieli dell'autunno mesti	56
Ora che dalla vita ad un ignoto	182
Ora gli alberi folti del viale	46

Ora ho chiesto a piú d'un savio	140
Pace dei campi, requie della morte	104
Pe 'l remoto viale di campagna	36
Per le città, nostre o d'oltralpe, in ogni	110
Perché sí bello han fatto il campanile	102
Pur tu me segui ancora, ombra dolente	158
Pure, il bene, io lo fo. Nel farlo, sento	168
Quand'ero al Reno... O amici miei Renani	88
Quand'io tornai d'un altro amor già stanco	160
Quando in croce Gesú l'anima rese	118
Quella giubbetta a maglia	90
Ricco jeri, oggi povero. E non so	86
Ride bagnato, addosso a la montagna	46
Rido se vedo un bimbo che la mano	174
Se con mano tremante (e già la mano	158
Segano l'afa le cicale. Acuto	108
Senza far nulla, un leone è leone	106
Silenzio. Gli altri, con le amiche a braccio	112
Smarrito, smarrito... A guardare	140
So che dovrei di ciò ch'è in terra solo	132
Sono a la mia finestra, al quinto piano	14
Sono, io dico, come un uomo che si sia	10
Sono stato a veder l'amico morto	100
Sperate di rimuovere ogni danno?	204
Sú, allegra, allegra, cara mia! Mi pare	116
Tele di ragno lavorate a maglia	66
Tengo a vantarmi solo d'una cosa	82
Un morto, e la campana non si lagna	50
Una mèta! una mèta! Ma sul ramo	74
Vedi tu come, non ancor dal fumo	142
Vivo del sogno di un'ombra nell'acqua	206
Volle pe 'l nido suo, pei nati suoi	42
Vuoi darmi la manina? Ti ci metto	178

Index of First Lines — English

A bell rings in everyone's heart	177
A death, and the bell does not lament	51
A goal! a goal! But may not the bird	75
And at last, here I am in port. My eyes	149
And from this brink I vainly seek again	187
And I said this to her more than once	157
And if not in you, neither may I seek	187
And should I really believe her, she's	199
And still I walk on	181
And this is the light that helps us see	193
At the entrance to life	71
At the gate of dreams where	135
But the Earth, if not beautiful	77
Cicadas pierce the sultry air. High-pitched	109
Come on, cheer up, my dear. I think	117
Dark days, weary days!	181
Dawn has waked you. Now that the fog	143
Drenched, the town perched on the mountain	47
Each fleeting moment teaches me	9
Easy to say, choose oneself a path!	139
Eternal eternal eternal!	23
Even if the vast mystery that leads you astray	191
Every now and then I raise my head from the pillow	165
He can't sleep 201	
Here is the globe: a cardboard ball	125
How truly wretched you are now	189
I am like the tree that waits	63
I can boast of one thing only	83
I feel watched by the stars	133
I have conceived the solemn doubt	139
I have seen ships set out for distant seas	171
I know that I should occupy my mind	133
I laugh when I see a baby open	175
I live in the dream of a shadow in water	207
I say that I am like a man who has	11
I was pulled down by violent blows	171

237

I would like it if pretty women	131
I'm at my window on the fifth floor	15
I'm here by chance, passing through	139
I've asked of more than one wise man	141
I've been to see our friend who died	101
If with a trembling hand — and already	159
In the cities where I sometime lived	111
It seemed to me, on those steep slopes	181
Let it go.... What does it matter?	175
Let's imagine that our Earth	81
Like a vast and placid serpent	137
Long hope and brief desires	131
Look at this crowd: priests and drunks	13
Look, winter, already dying	35
Lost, lost...I stand	141
Maybe because I look at its tearful	155
Meanwhile in the darkness, where many people	191
My days slip by as if gathered	9
My duty is this: to pass	195
My neighbor, on an April morning	97
No, for if I do not somehow fill the void	185
Now that I can no longer throw an airy	183
Now the thick trees along the road	47
O ancient Earth, it's true, and I regret it	121
O chestnut trees in the woods, you make	39
Of the foreigner who still has the sun of his homeland in his eyes	29
On a remote country path	37
On the hammock, suspended between	53
On the horizon the sky is enveloped in fire	177
Only a few leaves, from time to time	49
Peace in the fields, the stillness of death	105
Rich yesterday, today poor. And I don't know	87
She chattered a lot	93
She wanted for her nest, for her newborns	43
She will understand, I thought, today or tomorrow	157
Silence. The others, sweethearts on their arms	113
So life seems to you	197
So you're alive also, as am I	109
Solitary house in the middle of my native	59
Specifically, what's your desire, what do you want?	147
Spider webs worked in the finest	67
Spinning, spinning...so many tops	77

Start walking 75	
Still, I do good. Doing it, I feel that	169
Still tied here, since that year	179
Take pleasure, oh my flesh, as long as the years	13
That knitted jacket	91
The bits of straw, trash in the street	175
The crescent moon sails slowly in the arcane	7
The first swallow darts from the nest	199
The land I once dreamed of, ignorant	3
The little almond trees, the saplings	41
The memorable night is now at hand	151
The mulberry tree? Gone. There's only	59
The trees that seemed so joyful in	57
The woods seemed made	91
This I would do: compose a single ode	19
Thus it is for of death alone that I	185
To no Power above or beyond my reason	189
To the violin trilling its heartfelt	67
We are not made to understand	79
What do I know of myself? I know what the times want	169
What have you done? Tell me, perhaps because	107
What's happening to me?	127
When I, already tired of another love, came back	161
When I was on the Rhine — O my Rhenish friends	89
When Jesus on the cross gave up the ghost	119
Who says that time passes?	207
Who'd like to buy my clouds?	5
Why was the bell tower so beautifully made	103
Will you give me your hand? I'll give you	179
Without doing a thing, a lion is a lion	107
Worn out, mute, under the fiery	55
Yet you haunt me still, sorrowful shade	159
You light the lamp in your sad room	163
You'd like to rid the world of all its ills?	205

☉ ☉ ☉

This Work Was Completed on September 21,
2016 at Italica Press, New York.
It Was Set in ITC Giovanni
& Printed on 55-lb.
Natural Paper.